THIRTY SECONDS
OF SILENCE

THIRTY SECONDS OF SILENCE

by Fereshteh Roshan

Charleston, SC
www.PalmettoPublishing.com

Thirty Seconds of Silence

Copyright © 2020 by Fereshteh Roshan

All rights reserved.

First Edition

Paperback ISBN: 978-1-64990-318-1

To my parents,
the champions of my life,
and to my brother Rahmat,
the guardian of my soul.

To my children,
and all immigrant children around the world.

Be generous in prosperity and thankful in adversity, Be fair in thy judgment, and guarded in thy speech. Be a lamp unto those who walk in darkness, and a home to the stranger. Be eyes to the blind, and a guiding light unto the feet of the erring. Be a breath of life to the body of humankind, a dew to the soil of human heart, and a fruit upon the tree of humility.

—Bahá'u'lláh

ABOUT THIS BOOK

I dedicate this book in loving memory of Mr. Rodney L. Johnson, a great man, a true friend, and a humble champion, whose encouragement, support, and provision inspired me to write about my life journey. Rodney was a great African American man who believed that my story reflected the lives of many African Americans, and that's why he encouraged me to get my story out. Hafiz, a great Persian poet, says, "The heart revived by the spirit of love will never die." That's how Rodney's pure love and joyful memories will be treasured and remembered as long as I live. I am forever grateful for his friendship and support.

You are free to judge this book by its cover. It's a picture of me at the age of five or six, when most parts of the story took place. The image of the field is a painting of our summer plantation, the place where our best childhood memories happened. We still dream about that meadow and treasure the memories we made there. I asked my brother Karim to paint an image of our summer home, and he kindly agreed. He also painted the back cover, but I will leave that story for you to discover. I admire Karim for his creativity, talents, and skills. He learned to paint on his own, with no specialized training.

You may love or hate this story; I don't mind. Love and hate, the two dominant forces of life, have granted me many privileges and lessons, and I learned to acknowledge and embrace them both as tools for growth. This book is the real story of me, and many other people like me, living our God-given lives. Writing this book was responding to a call, and I feel the obligation to those I lost over the course of this journey to get their voices out. I have changed many of the main characters' names for their protection. I hope one day we can step out of the fears and concerns and speak freely.

Simplicity is one of the major scales used to measure the quality of almost everything, whether it's fashion design, industry innovation, or even basic conversation and writing. Simplicity is often the primary key to accomplishing things better, no matter how intelligent and skillful we are. I remember when I was a young girl and wanted to put makeup on or dress up like the other young girls without even thinking whether that style looked good on me, my mama would say, "Simplicity is the only one style that never wears out; no matter what comes on the market as a trend, there's always a simple version of it out!" Today I know she was right, and I've tried to listen to this one piece of her advice for nearly thirty years. I've always tried to stay simple in life and in all its matters.

English is my second language, and I started learning it in my late twenties when I came to the United States nineteen years ago. I can bravely say I learned much of my English through my two children growing up here. It was hard to keep up with them after they passed secondary school. So be patient with me, and pay attention to the essence of my story rather than the structure of it and the script of the text. I am not planning to leave a masterpiece in English literature; I know my limits and boundaries, and I admit my imperfections in many ways.

I would like to take this opportunity to thank my two children for checking some parts of this book. However, after few chapters, I decided not to reveal the entire story to them, as I meant to leave them the gift of a lifetime. This book is a gift to my children and to all immigrant children who faced challenges at their young age all around the world.

A strong scene in a play can carry a valid message even without the best set or stage design. The message of this book is what matters to me. It's a humble story of my simple rural family life. This might be my last walk on the "edge of blades," and if that's the case, I am willing to take that final walk with grace.

PREFACE

A STRANGE HOMELESS MAN

August 2016, Shenandoah, Virginia. I had accompanied my fifteen-year-old daughter to a youth summer camp. It was her first year attending that camp. Most of the camp activities focused on preparing youth to face the social and environmental challenges of the future and to gain knowledge and skills for better communication. There were also some workshops to engage parents while the kids attended their classes. I noticed a homeless man among us. I was not sure if he was a parent of any of the children, or if this instructive event was important for a person like him to attend.

The homeless man kept walking around and collecting recyclables. He was even digging in trash cans and separating the recyclable materials. I assumed he was a local man who was hanging around looking for scraps. The first night of our arrival, the children and parents gathered in the auditorium for a brief introduction to the camp program and to socialize to some live music. At the end, each family went to their rooms.

The next morning, the parents were divided into small groups based on our various interests. There were eight people in my group, including me. Surprisingly, the homeless man was in our group. Our assignment was focused on community-building actions such as helping the well-being of each of our neighborhoods and planning to build a safe, unified, and cohesive environment for our children to grow in. We studied some preselected articles, discussed the different scenarios and issues we were facing in our communities, and practiced different ways to solve them.

As we went through the introduction part, I got a better chance to observe the homeless man. I noticed he had many rings. I wondered how come he had so many, almost enough to have two on each finger. Those rings looked expensive. He introduced himself as John. To be honest, I didn't get the rest of what he had to say. His choice of vocabulary was too hard for me to comprehend. When we got to the consultation part, I found him to be a very knowledgeable, confident, and intelligent man. Boy, he knew almost everything! He was full of ideas, viewpoints, experiences, and theories. I was in awe watching him for the next eight hours of the workshop. What amazed me was the fact that even between the breaks, he would walk around and collect recyclables from trash cans!

In the afternoon, when the activities for kids and adults were done, I saw him sitting peacefully in a rocking chair on his porch, watching the sunset. I said hello and asked him if it was OK that I sat next to him. He grabbed me a chair and said, "Sure, please!" Our conversation began about the workshop we had earlier and the neighborhood we'd come from. I told him a little but not much about my family and my background. Then I waited for him to speak and to tell his secret. Why would an intelligent, educated man who was born in the United States and spoke perfect English choose this type of lifestyle? Speaking English by itself is one of the most critical requirements for any person in the United States. If someone has no problem communicating in English, then they must not have any problems at all.

He was a retired educator with three master's degrees. Although he didn't mention the names of his fields of study, I assumed they were social, environmental, or economic, based on the discussions at the workshop earlier. He said he'd visited over thirty-five countries and had learned a lot about peoples of different cultures. He said during his extensive traveling around the world, he'd experienced countless similarities and connections between different cultures, and that made him wonder if a unified identity, a universal truth, or a common call could ultimately unite the people of different cultures together, something that could change their focus from forming divisions to building connections. We all have experienced that desire at different times and levels—a void, a space between where we are now and the point where we belong.

John said, "My search ended two years ago when one of my neighbors invited the rest of the neighbors to their home. We'd known each other for many years, but like most neighbors, we never had a conversation about matters besides our regular daily dialogues. That night we watched a documentary on YouTube together that changed my vision. The video was of a large and diverse community in Colombia that used a unique approach to help the people rise above their disagreements and personal interests. It enabled them to lay out a unique plan to resolve their local issues, like racism, children's education, the economy, the general health and well-being of the environment, and many more matters that experts don't have a practical resolution to yet.

"The plan worked through the spirit of fellowship and teamwork, the sense of selflessness, and mutual enthusiasm. As the result of their efforts, that town was able to bring unity, safety, joy, and prosperity to all. No military force! No government interference! No additional budgeting and investing, and no failure!

"That vital fundamental force, the spirit of love and real bonding, and the integrity in aiding one another were the missing pieces of the puzzle, and it became my quest. In the end, that video suggested a new vision of human destiny, a new era of a lasting peace and unity on our planet."

He then continued, "Can you believe this idea, that unique culture of peace and harmony, has been practiced everywhere for almost two hundred years, yet no one talks about it here? I had to make a few more travels to different places, including my homeland, Germany, to see if anybody knew or practiced that global culture. I was surprised to see that phenomenon had been practiced on every corner of the earth, including my own homeland. Seeing many of my people committed to that distinct faith, I would say I found myself as a new believer in world citizenship at home."

He took a long pause and then continued with assurance in his voice, "I have lived over sixty-five years, but the last two years of my life count as my true existence. It all starts with basic communication. We live like strangers now. No one knows what the next person is going through. I am so mad; I was searching for that answer for many years, and my next-door neighbor had it." He said with a little irritation, "I am so mad at him, because he never took time to tell me what he believed and practiced in all those years of our friendship."

He then asked me, "Why don't you speak up and share your story?"

I was not prepared for that question. How did he even know about my story? I responded, "Well, you know, I am an Iranian immigrant here, and I still have a lot to learn. I have nothing to offer."

He responded, "I am sure you have a good story to tell. That's the reason you are here in the United States. Isn't that right?"

"Yes, it is, but it's a different culture," I said. "People may not get my story."

He replied with frustration in his voice, "That's the exact reason I am mad. We judge people before we even talk to them, and that judgment blocks us from knowing each other. That's why we are suffering. There is a silent genocide happening back in your homeland, Iran; they are killing your people, and yet you are afraid some people may not get it?"

He was an experienced educator, and I'm sure he was concerned about some unpleasant facts around the globe, like war, injustice, racism, violence, human rights, and many more issues, but I could not imagine my story even mattered to him or that he knew anything about it.

He gave me some time to grasp what he had to say. The concern he expressed was powerful. He was making some points using facts about my people and their challenges. After a few moments of silence, he repeated with an ache in his voice, "I've seen enough of what our planet is going through. Speak up, or write your story down; that's how you can help your people back home. People need to hear about your story!"

I was no longer curious about his way of dressing; that didn't even matter anymore. I was not the same person after that short conversation. He changed my perspective by pointing out those crucial facts about my challenges and my past. I thanked him and said goodbye to prepare for the evening programs that had been arranged by the youth earlier in the day.

That night at the auditorium where all the parents and their children had gathered, I saw John standing in a corner. I walked over to him and introduced my daughter to him. I told him, "If I asked you to give my daughter one piece of advice, what advice would that be?"

He looked directly in her eyes. After a few moments, he said three words only: "Study your roots!"

Those were the most potent three words I've ever heard. My children came to the United States at a very young age. Like most immigrant children, they faced some challenges growing up in a different culture. My job as a parent was to understand them and help them learn and grow in their new home. They might not get the experience of the story I've lived, but I'm sure one day they will be able to connect strongly with their roots.

That piece of advice he gave me has always been in the back of my mind: "Speak up, and write your story down." I couldn't find the mystery behind his style; that might be a secret that I may never know, and that's OK. I heard what I needed to hear. Later on I heard his story from a friend, and it sent chills down my spine.

INTRODUCTION

YALDA CELEBRATION

December 2018, Herndon, Virginia. It was the night of Yalda, one of the most ancient Persian festivals, celebrated on the longest night of the year, December 21. That's the date that marks the point when nights start to shrink shorter and days start to grow longer. Yalda celebrates the arrival of winter, the renewal of the sun, and the victory of light over darkness. Many countries, like Iran, Afghanistan, Tajikistan, Uzbekistan, and Turkmenistan, and some Caucasian states, like Azerbaijan and Armenia, share the same tradition of celebrating Yalda. Red and green are the original colors of Yalda. I noticed here in the United States those are the same colors of Christmas, and Yalda is celebrated only a couple of nights before Christmas Eve.

Friends and families get together around some stunning *korsis*. A *korsi* is a low, round table covered by a large Persian-patterned tablecloth. We can easily sit on the floor around the *korsi*. Sometimes a small traditional charcoal heater keeps our feet warm under the *korsi*. On top of this stunning traditional table, we put flowers, red candles, and colorful seasonal fruits, like pomegranates, watermelons, and berries, and also some dried fall fruits and nuts.

Gathering around on the floor represents humbleness, unity, fellowship, and joy. Yalda is the rebirth of the sun, and we celebrate it by singing songs and reciting poems by the great Persian poet Hafiz. Yalda is a perfect time to get some advice from Hafiz. His poems guide you to understand life better. Although they can be recited at almost any occasion, Yalda is a particular night for Hafiz!

We were gathered in the beautiful house of our close friends, Mina and Farid, with almost twenty-five other people. The table was set beautifully. The dinner was fantastic; the vibe and energy were so uplifting. We had so much fun singing, laughing, and dancing. The men played games at another table while bragging about their luck and superior skills in defeating their opponent. Young girls and boys were playing and laughing. Women still sat at the *korsi*, telling funny stories about their children and husbands. Everyone looked well groomed and joyful, just like on Christmas Eve.

One of the women suggested that Bruce, one of the guests, knew a little about palm reading. We had known him for some time. He was a retirement-aged man who sat quietly in the corner, observing everything. He spoke only when someone started a conversation with him or asked him a question. I knew he was an educated man who had written some articles for newspapers. I had also read a few of his poems before. But reading palms?

Some people believe in palm reading, and some don't. I had never tried it before, since I'm not a believer. As the women gathered around him, asking about the possibility of him reading their palms, he made it clear that he was not a palm reader or fortune-teller, and this was not one of the regular activities he practiced. Bruce said he had done some research about palm reading while he was a college student, and he'd done it just out of curiosity back then. But those women insisted, and at last he agreed, saying, "I am doing it just to pass some time tonight." The ladies agreed.

I watched him as he read almost everybody's palm. Most of the points he addressed were general knowledge about each person, but sometimes he paused, made some encouraging recommendations, and gave words of advice. You could tell that he was an experienced man and didn't want to say anything unrealistic. He was basically guiding each person in a positive direction as he pointed to some truths. It looked more like a life-coaching or counseling session.

I was the last one at the table. He started to observe my palms for a few minutes, and it took so long for him to say a word. He was studying my palms like he was reading a map from all directions. I looked at friends, smiling and waiting to hear another broad statement. He moved his glasses on his nose and said with concern in his voice, "You lived only for the first six years of your life. You've been walking on the edge of blades since then."

That was harsh to hear. I said, "You mean eggshells?"

He said, "I mean blades."

I was not sure how to respond to that statement, and I was curious to know what he meant. I looked at him inquiringly, and he continued, "People either love you or hate you for who you are."

Looking at my past experience, I knew he was right! But Yalda was all about joy and enjoyment, and I just wanted to make it a fun conversation, so I asked him teasingly, "That sounds serious. What should I do, then?"

He looked directly into my eyes and, with confidence in his voice, said, "Start writing your story. It's worth hearing."

He left me puzzled and confused by that short, straightforward statement. I hadn't expected to hear it on such an entertaining night. Yalda was a chance to forget all about our pains and conflicts and to enjoy our time.

The palm reading didn't matter; what's important was the remarks he made at the end. That particular conversation reminded me of the one I'd had with John about two years ago. They both gave me momentum, a force and sense of obligation by advising me to write my story. I suddenly remembered the conversation I'd had with my mother years ago. When I told her over the phone that I was planning to write our family story, her response was, "I'm afraid it's too late. Baba is gone." I got an uneasy feeling. I felt the urgency to fulfill that promise before Mama was gone as well. That was an awakening moment for me, and I felt I had to start writing my story. You may love or hate my story, but I need to tell it.

1

MY CHILDHOOD

"Quit putting baby clothes on those poor chickens. Leave them alone," said Mama as she carried a brazier of flaming charcoal inside the summer cabin to get dinner ready. It was a mild summer afternoon, and the sun was getting ready to set behind tall, generous mountains. We had played all day long, and we were tired. We started taking the baby clothes and skirts off the chickens. My seven-year-old sister, Golara, and I had put on a fashion show with those chickens, and we'd laughed for hours watching them walking and grazing. I was six years old, and I enjoyed playing with my sister. Although we had many chickens, only three of them were our pets and had names. My chicken, Pa-Pary, was a chubby, black-and-white bird with feathers on her legs. Baghali was a tall, slim chicken with reddish-brown polka dots; she belonged to Golara. My eleven-year-old brother, Karim, had a reddish rooster named Ka-Koli. To be honest, now that I think back, those chickens looked just like us three.

Karim led the chickens into their coop and made sure the entrance door was secured. A couple nights ago, jackals had taken some of our neighbors' chickens. Our farms were so extensive that no fence or boundary was enough to protect our animals or us. This was the place where humans and animals learned to coexist. There were many kinds of animals inhabiting this vast meadow. We saw snakes, scorpions, lizards, and all types of big bugs, like beetles, and of course many kinds of birds during the day. But nighttime was the animals' domain here, and we just heard their howling and growling. There were foxes, jackals, wolves, boar, and deer, and it was said even panthers lived on top of the mountains. My father owned a portion of the territory called Palangan, which directly translates to panthers' land. In the past, many Iranian tigers lived in the region, but today only a few remain there. It was a forty-five-to-sixty-minute trip to that region from our summer location. I had overheard my father and his friends' conversations a few times about the times they'd gone hunting for deer and seen a *palang*.

One early morning, one of our neighbors, Javid, had dragged the body of a big wildcat, perhaps a cougar, to our cottage. He was proud of how he'd been able to take that cougar down for making trouble for their animals. We had heard its growling from a distance the previous night, but we didn't know it had actually attacked Javid's animals.

In spite of all the issues of this sort, this place was a serene place, and all creatures learned to live and enjoy a peaceful and harmonious life together as long as their nature allowed them.

Mama headed out to get some fresh water from the creek to make tea before Baba came back from the mountains. She told us to go with her and wash our hands and faces and to get ready for dinner. She told Karim to let the lizard go. That lizard was Karim's imaginary cow; he had used it to plow his little pile of wheat today. Watching that lizard run so fast and stir and spill all that wheat around had made us laugh so hard. It was nothing like a calmly chewing cow. Karim loosened the string around the lizard's neck carefully and set it free, knowing tomorrow he would find some other amusing toys in nature to play with. The lizard scuttled away without even looking back.

Sometimes Karim caught a big shiny beetle and tied a very thin string around one of its back legs, then joined all the other boys who prepared and trained for the Race of Flying Beetles. He had to take good care of that beetle and keep it in good condition—healthy, shiny, and energetic. He got it to practice a few times before the actual tournament started. This was a significant tournament that happened in summers only. They bet on winning beetles and traded them based on their agility, score, size, and color. Sometimes they trade them for other items like a good slingshot, or even a decent jaw harp.

Girls, on the other hand, had their own tournament, called Rig-Ghotour, or Raining Rocks. It's a game with unlimited levels that start with two sets of three rocks, six rocks in total. The number of sets grows as the players move to the upper levels. At the last few levels of the game, they have to play with fifteen to twenty sets of rocks—about forty-five to sixty rocks for each person. This game requires a lot of calculation, attention, and hand-eye coordination. The girls have to manage their own rocks while their opponent lays almost the same number of rocks on the field. Just throwing and shuffling those rocks is a difficult skill that I never got a chance to learn.

The older girls would allow us younger ones to start with a much simpler game called Yek-Ghol, Do-Ghol, meaning One Chain, Two Chains. This simple game has up to twelve chains or levels. You need only five rocks to play the primary game. This simple game is the base to prepare you for the big tournament. The girls walk around the patches of the meadow to handpick every single stone. Each rock is unique; no matter how many players race or how many stones are played, each person knows every single rock she has collected. It's like each piece of rock has a story behind it, and the girls grow a strong bond with those storytellers of nature. Some of those stones even have a special charm or attraction. The girls can get a handful of other rocks by trading with those special ones.

These tournaments were not the only games boys and girls participated in when I was a child. There were a lot of creative team games that boys and girls played without any specific toy, or they could simply create their own toy if they needed to. We had a quiet little cultural life as kids. We had our very own musical band. Each kid grabbed a bucket and two sticks, and we played music and sang for hours. Some older kids even created their own flute using hollow bamboo sticks or made some instruments by wrapping strings around some metal buckets. The jaw harp was something we had to get from the market, and almost everyone had one. And Baba made a set of swings for us using chains on a big walnut tree, making our official playground.

Sometimes we had to face some critical matters in our young group. I remember the time when we lost our little bird, Rana, an oriole. Orioles live on the fig farms and eat figs and tiny insects. They sing and can imitate different rhythms; they don't mimic words, just the rhythms. Rana was an excellent companion to my thirteen-year-old brother, Rahmat, who was blind. That bird was his wholehearted companion. While we were running and playing, Rahmat would carefully roam throughout the field with Rana sitting on his shoulder. They traded some of the rhythms that Rahmat practiced at his music school. He was the only kid among us who played an actual musical instrument, the *tar*. He played the tar very well, and he had such a heavenly voice. A tar is a string instrument very similar to a guitar but smaller and bulkier, and perhaps more complicated. Rana picked up some of those rhythms and imitated them. Rahmat was so sad at losing Rana. To give Rahmat a little comfort, we called all our cousins and neighbors' children on that day and conducted the most proper and respectable funeral we could hold for a companion bird like Rana. We were just practicing life as children in this peaceful meadow, Singing Willows.

2

SINGING WILLOWS

The name of this massive land was Bid-Bekhan, meaning singing willows, and it will be our ultimate reunion place if there is another life after this life. We still love and adore that place, although we don't own it anymore. There are three massive willow trees at the foothills of the mountains where the spring of cold, clear, fresh water surfaces from under the ground. When the wind blows between the branches of the willows, the melody mixes with the sound of spring water, and you can hear the most tranquil melody that nature can offer. It's all about peace and harmony there. The aroma of the wild herbs and flowers that cover the tall, generous mountains gives an exceptional flavor and feeling to the running stream.

My grandpa Agha-Mirza-Husayn, meaning Grandpa and Master Husayn, was a poet of his time; I called him Agha-Husayn. He had great handwriting, and he carved many Persian poems on stones at every corner of the lands he owned. At the very top of the spring, there is a large rock, and on it he carved this poem: "O travelers, who wander on this land with wonder. This is a fragment of heaven, if you ponder." I think that best represents Singing Willows.

Our grandfather left this piece of heaven for his four sons and his only daughter, Aunt Keyhan. The area was so vast that each of his children got at least few acres of the land. Mountains and creeks ran through it, and it would take us quite some time to walk to our neighboring aunts and uncles to visit, but that was not a problem. We all met at the shore of the spring, where pomegranate and walnut trees stood tall.

As the summer sunshine eased down, and three of us followed Mama toward the creek, we saw our aunts and cousins arriving at the shore. While moms and older children began greeting each other and sharing about their day, children ran around, climbed trees, and played hide-and-seek.

A little pond created by the running stream was the primary source of our drinking water. Moms filled their *koozeh*, big pitchers made out of clay, before they allowed children to the shore. The pond was about two feet deep, and it was so clear that you could count the little rocks on its floor. We got to drop some fresh fruits like figs, grapes, and pomegranates in the running water and let them cool off. We then sat around the pond and enjoyed those fruits, with our feet in the cold water. The water ran through wild Middle Eastern herbs and picked up the essence of the herbs, especially the mountain's wild mint, giving a distinctive taste and aroma to the fresh fruits we tossed in. This particular place was our daily family reunion site. Moms scraped pots and pans and washed clothes while waiting for their husbands and older sons to arrive at the shore, and kids still got to run around and play. Baba would be home soon.

I remember when Baba arrived, he would put one of us younger ones on his shoulders and pick up the other one. He then said, "Let me see if you've had enough food today." Golara was one year older than I, but I weighed more. My parents had always had a hard time feeding her. To inspire her to eat, Baba would put us in each tray of a large scale that was used to weigh large packs of almond and figs. I would always be stuck on the ground, and Golara would fly all the way up. She was very excited about going that high, and I always wanted to go up. Baba would then add some measuring stones to her side to balance out the scale so we both could swing and be happy. He then counted those stones and told her, "This is how much extra food you need to eat," but the excitement of being up so high obscured that entire trick for her. It never occurred to me that perhaps this was how much less food I should eat to get up there.

Nightlife at Singing Willows was very different. As I said before, it was the animals' kingdom after dark, and we learned to keep our space and know our limits. Right after sunset, we could hear hundreds of jackals howling down from the mountains. Baba said they were thirsty. They called each other down the mountain to drink water. They were harmless to humans, and we knew that we needed to give them their territory back. When we woke up in the morning, we could see their paw prints only a few feet from where we slept. They would eat our food or catch our chickens without making any noise. They walked so silently. It was almost impossible to hear their footfalls. I always wanted to see one of them, so I tried to stay awake many nights, but I always fell asleep and was never able to see one closely.

We could also hear wolves howling once in a while, especially around midnight. They never made any official group announcement like the jackals. Foxes were the next creatures that made noise sometimes before sunrise, and they didn't move in big groups either. Lizards, scorpions, mice, and snakes had their own field. They would leave you alone as long as you acknowledged their existence and respected their boundaries. Mice were funny; they worked so hard to steal our almonds. If you found their nests, you would be surprised to see how much they had collected in their storage. They could store around five kilograms of almonds.

My mama told us a funny story about how two mice once made an effort to steal one of the chicken eggs. She said, "One of the mice grabbed an egg tightly while lying flat on its back. The other mouse started to pull its tail all the way to their den, but the egg was too big to get through the entrance of their house." We laughed so hard picturing the mice planning this great heist. We created a reenactment playing the two mice working hard to steal the egg.

The sky of Singing Willows was a deep blue during the day and dark and luminous at night. The city, which we lived in during the school year, didn't have that bright a sky. It was due to the city lights outshining the stars. The sky of the meadow was fascinating and mysterious to watch, and we enjoyed the stories Mama told about the stars. She knew the names of many stars and the tales people had told about them. Every night we fell asleep watching those bright stars and listening to Mama's or Baba's stories. Once you connect with the beauty and the mystery of the sky, you will always be bonded to it. Sometimes we could see a shooting star, and we made a wish.

Some nights our relatives would gather at our cabin. There was not enough space for everybody inside, but there was unlimited flat valley under the moonlight outside. Everybody got their lanterns and came to our cabin. They came for two reasons: Baba was the eldest son in his household, and it's a tradition to get together at the elder members' homes; also, our parents felt it was not safe to walk Rahmat to other places at night.

Just like our grandfather, Rahmat had a heavenly voice. His presence would add so much joy and comfort to our gatherings. He would sing Hafiz's poetry and play the tar, while others appreciated him and sipped their tea around the fire. Kids were exhausted at this point. We preferred not to leave the crowd, so we played games that didn't require running around or making much noise.

In the early morning, before the sun was out, Baba turned on the radio that hung from the ceiling of the cabin. I remember waking up every morning to the confident and powerful voice of Jaffar, Shir-e-Khoda, singing ancient Bastani verses to encourage exercise and bodybuilding. Bastani is an ancient sport that combines martial arts with heroic poems and music that is played on special drums like those used on battlefields.

Just like his father, Baba had a strong and assertive voice. I loved hearing Baba chant prayers early, at every sunrise. His voice gave me a sense of reassurance and love. Listening to such a strong man and seeing him kneel so humbly and pray at the sunrise was a powerful experience.

Our grandpa must've been an extraordinary man. I heard from Baba that he had a magnificent voice. When the summer season was over and everyone was back into town, Agha-Husayn would conduct poetry nights. He would recite parts of the famous epic poem *Shah-Nameh*, or *Book of Kings*, by a great Persian poet, Hakim Ferdowsi. Baba said he remembered accompanying his father to almost every poetry night he conducted.

I heard stories of how knowledgeable and respected Agha-Husayn was among his people. He was one of the few people of his time who were able to read and write. He was not an official mullah, but the way people looked at him told how much respect they had for him.

I never met Agha-Husayn. He passed away many years before I was born. In fact, none of his many grandchildren got a chance to meet him, but those meaningful poems that he carved into enormous stones all over Singing Willows made strong bonds and connections. It felt like he never left us, especially given the fact that those poems pointed to the people who would live on that land after him, his children and grandchildren. We felt his presence all the time.

I could imagine how Agha-Husayn looked. To me, he was a medium-to-tall, muscular man. He was definitely shorter than my baba. I imagined he had tanned skin, almost like leather. He had the most beautiful blue eyes a Middle Eastern man could have. He had a full, dark-blond mustache and a rough, short beard. I could even picture his facial lines and wrinkles, especially his smile lines—that was how all his four sons looked. I can say they were the best-looking men in that region.

The four brothers and their only brother-in-law built their summer cottages at the foothills of the mountains. Many other people were living near the next few acres from us, and they would get together for special occasions once in a while. We spent our summers at Singing Willows working and recharging for when we moved back to our town at the start of the school year. Singing Willows was indeed a piece of heaven, and we appreciated it dearly.

3

LIFE IN THE TOWN

Our town, Neyriz, was located in the southeastern province of Fars, Iran. It's a three-hour drive from Shiraz, the capital city of Fars. Mountains surround the town, and the four seasons take their complete terms there. Pleasant warm weather during the summer and a moderate to cold winter give the area a complete balance. Spring was the most beautiful season in our town, since orchards of blossoming fruit trees, like apricots, peaches, cherries, and plums, grew there.

At the beginning of fall, people who'd been working on their plantations outside the town returned home. I loved that transition; life would never get boring. We lived in the same neighborhood as all of our cousins. We spent most of our time playing and going to school together. Our games and activities would change, since we couldn't run wild in the town, and we also had schoolwork to do. We always managed to enjoy and treasure our time together. I remember when our maternal grandparents, Agha-Mirza-Hassan and Bebe-Golnaz, went to visit their only son, Uncle Behzad, in Shiraz for a few weeks. We had such a blast playing in their yard. Their house was right next to ours, and we had access to the yard only. Mama could check on us anytime.

I remember one afternoon there were almost fifteen of us kids playing there. I was the youngest of the group, perhaps five or six years old. I was sitting in a large *joughan*, a massive, bowl-shaped pot made out of stone. I believe it's called a mortar in English. They used it to grind significant amounts of seeds and kernels like wheat, oat, or *banneh*, wild pistachios. They also made the most delicious home-made sweets by crushing almonds and dried figs together to make a soft and creamy paste. A mixture of coconut and sugar was also one of my favorite treats.

As I was playing and moving inside the *joughan*, the air compressor around my back made a funny noise, and I was amused by it. I sat in there and played for quite some time. I was not paying attention to see that the older kids were getting ready to leave. I was trying to get myself out of the *joughan*, but I was stuck, and no one could hear me. Everyone was laughing and talking as they left, drowning out my cries for help. I was so anxious about getting left behind. A six-year-old child stuck in that huge yard right before sunset—what would I do if jackals came for me? What if a scorpion or snake bit me? What if I never saw my mama and baba again?

After a few minutes, I managed to get myself out of the stone bowl. Walking out on the verge of tears, I heard my brother Karim say, from the top of a long brick wall behind me, "Psssst!" My other two cousins, Amir and Habib, twelve and thirteen, were on the wall with Karim too. They motioned for me to keep quiet and swung down a long rope to me. Karim held the other end of the rope and whispered for me to look at him and do exactly what he was doing. He tied the other side of the rope around his waist, instructing and watching me do the same. I did all the steps very carefully. He made more knots around his waist to be safe, and I copied him. In the end they dragged me all the way up the wall. Karim kept the other end of the rope tied around his waist the entire time, in case our cousins couldn't drag me up. When I got on top of the wall, I asked, "Wait a minute, what happened to the key? You could have simply opened the front-yard door and let me out. Why did you have to drag me up the wall like that?"

Karim replied, "We already handed the key back to Mama, and I couldn't tell her that I left you behind! You know she would get upset."

Now that I think back to that particular event, I see how many elements worked together to save me: teamwork, responsibility, willingness to take a risk, and keeping secrets, but most of all love! Just the fact that Karim kept the other end of the rope around his waist during those tough few minutes told me how much he loved and cared for me. He was willing to risk his own life to save me that evening. I felt I was the luckiest little sister. I didn't tell Mama about it until a few days ago. She is eighty-six years old now and had a good laugh hearing it.

In addition to the regular public schools we attended, we joined another school every Friday morning. It was called Dars-e-Akhlagh, school of virtues, a home-based virtue instruction for Baha'i children that is practiced all over the world. Among the fifteen kids in our big extended family, Karim, Golara, and I were the only ones attending that school; some kids from other neighborhood areas would join, but no one else from our family. Sometimes our cousins showed up, but not often. I remember one day, the three of us had a serious conversation with Mama regarding that school. Karim, who was older, asked Mama, "How come we are the only ones who go to the school of virtues? Why don't our other cousins go with us?"

"Because they are not Baha'i," Mama replied.

I knew that we were Baha'i, but I never realized that the rest of our relatives were not. The rest of Karim's conversation with my mama went like this:

Karim: "How come we are the only ones who are Baha'is?"

Mama: "Among all of Agha-Husayns children, Baba was his only child who decided to accompany him when he was studying. The rest of his children were comfortable where they were."

Karim: "How about our grandma Bebe Maryam? Is she Baha'i too?"

Mama: "She is the most loving, caring, Muslim grandma anybody could ask for." Mama was right; Bebe Maryam was the most adoring, affectionate, sweet grandma. She loved all of us dearly, and we were so lucky to be her grandchildren.

Karim: "How come Agha-Husayn was Baha'i and his wife was not?"

Mama: "Agha was Muslim too! He became Baha'i in the later years of his life. He started searching for the signs that most religions confirmed as the coming of the 'Promised Day,' and he found those signs in the Baha'i faith."

Karim: "How come those clerics and mullahs who were studying and reading all the time didn't see it?"

Mama: "Most of the people, including clergy and priests, who are genuinely looking for the truth will find it. But the question is if they want to accept the truth. Some leaders choose not to accept it."

Karim: "Why not?"

Mama: "They study only their own book. Some of them are even afraid God will punish them for considering another book or idea. They are worried if people convert to other beliefs, they will lose patrons. They even threaten people about asking questions or getting close to us."

Karim: "But why, Mama? Don't we believe in Islam? Do we have anything against them?"

Mama, smiling: "My dear son, we don't have anything against any religion. We believe and respect all messengers of God. In fact, as a Baha'i, your love and respect for other prophets and manifestations of God grows even stronger. One of the elements of being Baha'i is to be open and loving toward all God's children, no matter what they believe and practice. The ultimate intention of the Baha'i faith is peace and unity among humankind."

Karim: "How come we have never seen a Baha'i cleric?"

Mama: "We don't have any clergy like a mullah, priest, rabbi, or any individual to rule others."

Karim: "But how do we figure things out without their help?"

Mama: "God created human intelligence, and that intellect brings us the capability and responsibility. We are all created equally, and no individual has the personal authority or power to control others, especially in the name of God. It is everyone's own mission to explore their path independently."

Karim: "How about the tough stuff that we can't figure out on our own?"

Mama: "With access to the resources, especially numerous scriptures and writings, and with the wisdom of consultation, you can find solutions for almost every problem."

Karim: "What do you mean by the wisdom of consultation?"

Mama: "I mean through a Local Spiritual Assembly."

Karim: "What is that?"

Mama: " A Local Spiritual Assembly consists of nine members who are elected every year by people of each locality to administrate the affairs of that area. The assembly functions as a body and makes decisions through devotion, dedication, and consultation. They practice the teachings in scriptures and writings to utilize the community's resources and ensure that the society advances to its full capacity."

Karim: "What exactly do they do?"

Mama: "Examples of their responsibilities are promoting the social and spiritual education of children and young people like you. They also strengthen the spiritual and social life of society, promote harmony and unity by sponsoring and supporting local and individual service projects to uphold the well-being of society, and support and enforce equity and justice for all people regardless. You may find it hard to understand now, but you will comprehend more as you get older."

Karim: "So, do those individuals rule as clerics and mullahs, then?"

Mama: "No! The Aassembly works as one unit on reviewing scriptures, searching resources, and making decisions with the spirit of consultation. The elected individuals have no influence or power over people; they are just average citizens living normal lives. The election recurs every year, and the individual members gain no title or profit."

Karim seemed to need some time to process what Mama had just explained to him. But he still wanted to know why we were the only children who got to go to the Baha'i school. We liked attending the school, but we could see now why our cousins treated us so differently in town compared to when we were at Singing Willows. We had a good time playing and living together in the mountains' hills, but our cousins could be cruel to us back in town, and they made sure people saw them differently. For example, they would go to Baha'i school with us on Friday, but the next day they were among other kids in the streets chasing us, throwing stones at us, and calling us names. It seemed in that small town, clergy motivated everyone against connecting or communicating with us, even our closest relatives.

Our cousins were wonderful people with good hearts, but they had to act so cruel in public because they were afraid if people considered them Baha'is, they'd treat them poorly, the way we were treated. I know it seems strange, but I felt sorry to see my cousins trying to protect themselves in such a cruel way. They loved us, and I know it was hard for them to treat us that way.

4

MY FAMILY

I've never seen a picture of my baba at a young age; he got married twenty-four years before I was born, when he was thirty-one. Although there was more than ten years' difference between him and my mother, I don't remember seeing a picture of my mother when she was young either. Perhaps that's the general view all children have of their parents—it's hard to imagine them as young people. But in my case, there were more than fifty-five years between Baba and me. I was their eighth and last child. They had five daughters: Sima, Nasim, Parvin, Golara, and me. They also had three sons: Reza, Rahmat, and Karim. Nowadays that might sound like a big family with too many children, but that was the standard number for a family a few decades ago, especially for the people who needed helping hands with farming.

My baba, Mirza'-Mohammad, was the eldest child of his family. When his father, Agha-Husayn, passed away many years ago, he became the head of his household. Perhaps that's the reason he got married so late!

Baba inherited all my grandfather's physical attributes: his facial features, his blue eyes, his tan skin, and his muscular build, in addition to his father's moral qualities. Just like his father, he was a well-known, respectable man with a good name around the town. As a matter of fact, he exceeded some of his father's qualities, like his braveness, his sharpness, and his confidence. People still tell stories about how he faced troubles when others seemed to be clueless. I witnessed it many times as a child and later in life. With his many good qualities, what I liked the most about him was the fact that he adored his wife, our mama, Zivar.

My mom was also the eldest child of her family. She was a tall and strong-built young girl with olive skin, black hair, and emerald-green eyes. She was also known for being bright, intelligent, and courageous, a girl who was brave enough to speak her mind yet gentle and caring enough to stand up for her relatives and neighbors when they felt troubled. She loved Persian poetry, especially the great poet Hafiz. She was a master in the old-style poetry reading called Fa'll-e-Hafiz. She used it to soothe and comfort people who felt anxious or concerned. You must acquire some knowledge of traditional Persian literature to be able to interpret Hafiz poems, *ghazals*. To help you know her better, I'll share a story that happened over sixty-five years ago, when she was just a young girl. I heard it when I arrived in the United States.

When I had just come to the United States, I participated in one of the regular community events at the Northern Virginia Baha'i Center. That night, I was honored to have a conversation with a sweet elderly lady, Mrs. Ahdy, who was in her eighties. After a few minutes of small talk, she asked where I came from, and I responded I was initially from Neyriz. She then asked, "Do you know Zivar, Mirza'-Hassan's daughter?

"Yes," I replied, "she is my mother."

Mrs. Ahdy was glad to meet me and said, "Look at you, how did I miss that? You look just like your mother." Then she asked how my mama was doing, and I told her that my father had recently passed away and she was still dealing with his loss. Mrs. Ahdy said a few words of condolence, then continued, "Your mother was a very brave and smart girl. I was a member of the Local Spiritual Assembly in Neyriz, when Zivar was just a young girl. Her father, Mirza'-Hassan, had become Baha'i. You know that's against the Islamic sharia."

"Yes, they could kill my grandfather."

"Exactly! There was a mullah called Seyed-Bisheh who put so much pressure on us on a daily basis. He would send us threatening messages that if we didn't stop teaching the faith, he would send some of his patrons to kidnap Mirza'-Hassan's daughter Zivar! He said that he would teach everyone a permanent lesson not to leave the sharia for the Baha'i faith. There was no legal source we could get help from."

I was shocked hearing such a story about my mother. I asked Mrs. Ahdy, "Then what happened to Zivar? Did they kidnap her?"

She smiled widely and said, "Never! We asked one of the boldest men of our town to guard her house and her family. His name was Mirza'-Mohammad, and I am sure he was able to take a good care of that family." She then looked down and said, "Unfortunately I had to leave the town, and I left Iran shortly after. I don't know what happened to them afterward."

I told her, "You did your job saving Zivar's life. She and Mirza'-Mohammad got married, and I am their last child."

She looked at me with joy in her eyes. She then asked, "Then your father must've become Baha'i too?"

"Yes! He has since become Baha'i."

I could tell she was dealing with mixed emotions, knowing my father had become a Baha'i after getting married, and that he had passed away not too long ago. That was an unforgettable conversation, and I will always remember that kindhearted lady.

Sima, the eldest of my siblings, was born nineteen years before me. She moved to Shiraz when I was one or two years old. She worked at the University of Shiraz as administrative staff and got married two years later at the age of twenty-two, when I was three years old.

Nasim and Reza, the second and the third children of the family, moved out to Shiraz shortly after Sima. They finished nursing school and started working at different hospitals. Nasim got married when I was four years old. She married a good-looking nurse who worked at the same hospital. Reza was twenty years old, living with Sima and her husband.

Parvin was seventeen at the time and also getting ready to move out, as her high school was finishing soon. As I mentioned before, my brother Rahmat was blind. He had to move to Shiraz before Parvin because there was no school or facility to help blind children to study in our town. He moved into the dormitory of a famous school called Shoorideh, a school specifically designed for blind students. That left three of us, Karim, Golara, and I, who were eleven, seven, and six years old, living with our parents.

It seemed we were a big family, but all eight of us almost never got to live together under one roof because of our age differences and the work and school situations of the older siblings. Four of them moved out shortly after I was born. We were two sets of four children with an age gap between the two groups.

Summer was a special time for our family because all our siblings and their families would come home and spend a few weeks at Singing Willows with us. It was terrific to have siblings of almost two different generations. I loved it, and I was so proud of my family. Our extended relatives would join us from different cities too, and we had an amazing family reunion in that charming meadow every summer.

5

A SCHOOL FOR THE BLIND

I remember being ecstatic to visit Rahmat at his school. His school was named Shoorideh, after the blind poet of Shiraz, Shoorideh Shirazi (1857–1923). The school was so unique, and we loved spending time there. It was a boarding school where students lived. Their classrooms were different from ours; there was no blackboard, no chalk, no pencils, and no erasers. Not even any pictures on the wall or in the books.

Braille, a method of reading and writing, is based on the finger-tips skimming raised dots on paper. The dots make up the letters of the alphabet, numbers, and punctuation marks. At Shoorideh they used a thick, light-brownish paper secured in a metal ruler, which had patterns of dots on it. To write, the students would use a special metal pen and the ruler's points to create pinholes on the paper. They also used a particular typing machine too, and when they typed in unison, you could hear a harmonic melody and a lot of ding-ding noises at the end of each line.

Unlike regular schools, Shoorideh had different workshops for learning arts and crafts like weaving, clay, even crochet and knitting for girls. You would be surprised how they succeeded and even excelled in almost every field, just like regular students. It's incredible how blind people develop their other four senses to fill the void for the loss of their eyesight.

Rahmat loved music, and there was a big department dedicated to music at his school too. They would teach students to play different Persian and Western instruments, as well as the history of music, including the various divisions and subdivisions of Persian music. Students would also take vocal lessons.

I remember a few years later, when I was almost ten years old and able to read and write, Rahmat asked me to help him label nearly two hundred audio tapes he had. He said some friends kept borrowing them and forgetting to bring them back. It was his very own music collection, and he wanted to label and organize them. I grabbed the tape player, assuming it would take at least three hours of our time to play and label those tapes. To be honest, I didn't want to sit there for three hours, but I settled in. Then Rahmat said he didn't need a tape player.

"How can you figure them out, then?" I asked.

He swiftly grabbed the first one, slipped the tape on his lower lip very smoothly, and said, "This is Banaa'n."

I wasn't sure, so I asked him, "Do you want to double-check with the tape player?"

"You can do it, but it won't be necessary."

I checked it, and he was right. I was in awe! We labeled almost every one of the tapes in only forty-five minutes without even playing them. Rahmat was the smartest kid in our household.

One day we arrived at their physical education class. They were playing soccer. I was so amazed to see how two teams of blind children were playing soccer, running after the ball without any problem. The trick was that they put a few small pebbles inside the ball, and as it rolled around, the pebbles made noise, and they followed it. For their teammates to determine their locations, they had to communicate by constantly shouting, "I'm here!" Like most complications in life, it seemed difficult at the beginning, but as they practiced and got a feel for the game, it became comfortable and fun for them.

Mr. Sa'dat, Rahmat's teacher, was very respectful and polite. The students loved him, and they were very comfortable around him.

He showed a lot of respect to the students and their families. He explained to my parents that, given the choice between home economics and art, Rahmat had chosen a bamboo-weaving class. But when the instructor saw his hands, he said those hands were too delicate for bamboo weaving. He suggested Rahmat try learning the tar. The teacher took our parents in his office to talk, and we had some time to spend with Rahmat. In spite of his disability, he was a hilarious and energetic older brother. He was good at imitating our favorite cartoon characters. He sang kids' songs and told our favorite stories. He was also excellent at playing the flute and playing the *tombak*, a Persian drum, while singing.

We played group games too. We played *esm-famil*, name games. One amusing game that he taught us was called *ki-koja-chikar*, meaning "who-where-what," an excellent game to play with your family and friends. We still enjoy playing the game at our gatherings. To play, each of us grabbed a piece of paper and a pen. The first player would list ten different people we all knew—relatives, neighbors, teachers, or even public figures. The second person would write a list of ten different small or big spaces, like on the table, inside a cup, in the shower, on the roof, and so on. And the third player would write a list of ten past-tense verbs or random actions. Then we took turns reading our first item on the list. It was so ridiculous to imagine that, for example, Uncle Rahim was brushing his teeth inside Baba's pocket. The game kept going until we read all items on the list in numeric order.

We had so much fun with Rahmat, but I always felt so sad that we had to leave him there and couldn't take him home with us. I could say Rahmat had the same feeling too.

6

THE FIRST YEAR OF SCHOOL

In September 1977, I was almost seven years old, and I was so excited about going to first grade that year. Mama got me some school supplies, including a little school bag, a small box of colored pencils, a set of red and black pencils to write with, and a brand-new notebook, which I didn't like. The color of its pages was not light and bright; I think the notebook was made from recycled paper. I also got a red strawberry-scented eraser that I loved to smell and sometimes taste secretly. I was the last kid of the household, and my parents were done getting excited about the first steps and the first days.

I had a fifteen-minute walk to school, and I was so excited. Mama walked Golara and I on the first day and watched us walking to school. Everything looked fine; the only strange thing was seeing a couple of kids screaming and crying while their parents almost dragged them to school. Seeing those children yelling and crying and running away made me think perhaps school was not a friendly place. I started to wonder if trusting my family about school was the right choice.

I remember a couple of times when Mama had offered to take us to the market and buy us cupcakes and ginger pastries. We got ready in a matter of seconds, and we were so excited about it, but we got confused seeing Mama pass by the pastry shop without buying any sweets for us. We'd ask her, "Why didn't you stop at the bakery?" and she'd reply, "We will get the cupcakes and the ginger cookies on the way back." When we heard that, we sprinted as fast as we could. She had to chase us all the way to the end of the market. Of course she would always get us some cupcakes on the way back from the doctor's office. That episode happened a few times, and we never learned our lesson. We always trusted Mama. Even when we had a slight idea of her plan for our doctor visit, we still felt safe in trusting her. Kids were much simpler back then.

The first day of school was not perfect but went all right. I didn't know anyone in my class, and I didn't know they would keep Golara in a separate classroom. I was excited about sitting in the front row, but they gave me a seat toward the back of the classroom. I thought I was not short enough to sit up front. I was able to make friends with only one of the two girls sitting by my side. One of them, named Khadija, was so annoying. She kept wailing loudly through every hour of the day, and I was tired of hearing her voice. Crying for the first few minutes or even an hour was acceptable, but she wouldn't stop crying at all. In spite of all of that, I was excited about going back to school on the next day.

A few weeks passed, and we were doing just fine. I liked my teacher, and I could tell she approved of me most of the time. I was an organized, quiet, and well-behaved student, and that was enough reason for my teacher to like me.

One afternoon I noticed Golara was so upset on the way back home. She was a small but energetic girl with beautiful green eyes and some cute freckles on her cheeks. She had burned her right palm a few days earlier, trying to help Mama make flatbreads on the wood-stove, and she had a bandage wrapped around her right hand. She never made any trouble for anybody at home or in school. She was a sensitive girl and very cautious not to bother anybody. Now she was crying quietly on the way back home. I knew she wouldn't tell me what was bothering her, and I didn't know what to do. When we got home, she explained to Mama how a few older kids had started bullying her at recess, right under Mrs. Zamani's watch. Mrs. Zamani was the assistant principal and had been working many years at that school.

Golara said the kids pulled her hair and pushed her onto the ground. She said she fell on her injured hand and started to cry because of the pain, but Mrs. Zamani seemed to be amused watching all that.

Mama knew Mrs. Zamani very well. She had been working at that school for many years, and our other siblings had had to go through the same problems with her. She'd been mistreating children and families like us for a long time. We just had to be patient and very careful not to cause any conflict during school. As a matter of fact, Mama had to go to school a few times and talk to her, but Mrs. Zamani had her own idea about our family and didn't want to change it.

The next day Mama walked us to school and went to the office directly to inquire about that incident. I asked Mama on the way back home what the matter was. Mama said, "Mrs. Zamani seemed to be upset because Golara has been asking questions that criticize the fundamentals of their beliefs, and she thinks Golara is doing it on purpose." She had told Mama that Golara was a bold and fearless girl, and she needed to know her limits. If she didn't quit asking those types of questions, they could expel her from the school. But Mama was so proud of Golara for asking those questions. Mama asked Mrs. Zamani to put her statement in writing and give it to her. Mama kept that letter for years. Limit your questions? We'd been taught to be brave, speak our minds, and ask questions, and this was just unfair and wrong, especially at school. School is the place for questioning and learning.

Going through years of public schools, I understood that there were some controversial ideas and beliefs that were preached to children and young adults. I don't want to call it brainwashing; it was more like a mixture of fear and obedience, with no questions permitted. We learned not to ask any forbidden questions around that matter. It would be safer if we just listened and didn't make any comments.

A few days went by after the incident with Golara, and I was not comfortable facing Mrs. Zamani. She started giving me that weird look too, and I didn't know why. It seemed like she knew something about me that I was not aware of, or she wanted to teach me a lesson too.

7

MY NEW NOTEBOOK

One day when I came home from the school, we received a package from my sister Nasim, who lived in Shiraz. In that package there was a notebook for me among several items for the family. It was not one of those recycled brownish notebooks; it was an actual bright-white notebook with a picture of a little bunny on it. I was so excited about my new notebook. I asked Mama if I could use it. She hesitated at first because I'd just gotten another brownish notebook, but even she couldn't resist it. She said, "OK, you can switch and use the other one later." I was so excited that afternoon. I did my best to write beautiful, neat, and clean home-work. Those couple of pages of homework seemed too good for a first grader to write. I was so proud of myself. I showed my homework to Mama and told her, "I will get a big-head score for this homework." I was elated to go to school the next day. I had a brand-new white notebook, and I'd written my homework beautifully on the first and second pages of it.

The school switched to a morning and afternoon shift every week, and that week was our afternoon shift. When I got to school, I was so disappointed to find our teacher hadn't come to work on that day. I got terrified when Mrs. Zamani walked into our class to cover for her. Then in my young mind, I began to think this was actually a good chance to change her view of Golara. I thought, "I have done my homework in the best way I could've, and I will do my best today to show her my school etiquette. When she asks me how I became such a good student, I will tell her that my sister Golara taught me all that. I will get a chance to tell her how good a person Golara is."

Mrs. Zamani reviewed some of our daily routines, like the posters we had on the walls, alphabet, numbers, and days of the week. She asked a few students to read yesterday's lesson. She then asked us to put our homework on our desks for her to view. As the she walked around each desk and reviewed our homework, I became increasingly uneasy. I had to get myself prepared for her arrival at my desk. She checked the homework of the person next to me and said nothing to her, although it wasn't neat and clean work. She then looked at my homework and said, "Who wrote that homework for you"?

I was horrified. I could hear my heartbeat. I replied with a weak voice, "I wrote it myself, *ejazeh*." *Ejazeh* is a term of respect, and it means "with your permission." It is a word students finish their sentences with when talking to a teacher.

She glared down at me for a long moment and then slapped my face so hard. I wasn't ready for that at all. I felt a strange ringing in my ears, and my eyes blacked out. She didn't even give me a chance to explain about my new notebook. She took a long, warm breath over my head and told me, "I've been teaching for over twenty-five years, and I can see a cheater from far away."

I felt so helpless! Tears started to stream down my little face, and I couldn't even say a word. She then called the office and asked our "school baba" to come and get me. Although I was in shock and very disappointed in her, I thought, "OK, she may ask him to drop me at home. I won't have to deal with her for the rest of the day." But she gave him another order. She told him to take me to a big storage unit at the very end of our schoolyard. She watched me as I wept, and she said, "Wipe those ugly blue spying eyes."

Our school baba was a good person. He and his family lived in a unit the school provided for a medium-sized family. They acted as the students' second family. Their job was very hard. In addition to cleaning and keeping the school organized, they helped teachers and students who needed assistance. They even sold snacks during recess for a reasonable price. Occasionally, if a student felt lonely and uncomfortable, they could spend a few minutes at the school baba's home, with the permission of their teacher, of course. Although school baba's wife was a caring, loving woman and like a second mama to the students, we never called her "School Mama." She was "School Stepmama." I don't know how that tradition came to be. I guess no one can take the place of your own mother.

The school baba grabbed my hand and took me to the storage unit. I had always wanted to see inside that storage. In my young imagination, behind that door there was a bright, colorful indoor playground with lots of toys and games, and I was hoping one day we could take a tour there or somehow I would be able to see inside of it. I never thought I would be dragged to that storage place for such an innocent and unfair reason!

He was acting like he was really upset with me while taking me to the storage. He blamed me loudly for not listening to my teacher. He said, "I cannot help anyone who doesn't listen to their teacher. You will learn a good lesson now." Hearing those words from him in that uncomfortable situation was so strange. When we arrived at the storage unit, he unlocked that huge iron door. The door opened with a loud, rusty sound. He pushed me inside, quickly jumped inside, and closed the door halfway.

His voice changed suddenly to a calm and comforting tone again, the tone I knew before. He spoke with a peaceful and kind voice. He said, "Don't worry, baba! I had to talk to you that way outside; they will fire me if I don't obey. You are safe here. As soon as the school closes, I'm going to run to your house and let your parents know you are here. Stay strong, and don't worry. I got your back." He then shut the door on me, locked it, and left.

Unlike in my imagination, the storage unit was a dark and cold place. I couldn't see anything. There was no window or light. After a few minutes, my eyes got used to the dark, and I could see my surroundings better. It was basically storage for broken desks and blackboards, nothing special to see. At least I got a chance to see inside that storage shed. After almost an hour, I started to get anxious. What if the school baba had lied to me? He was screaming and shouting at me outside the shed, and he was kind and calm inside it. How did I know which act reflected his true intent? He worked for the principal and he could get fired, so what gave him reason to risk his job to help me? What if they all forget about me, and snakes and scorpions came for me? I was in the same position as I was in Bebe-Golnaz's yard. I wished Karim was here to get me out.

As those negative thoughts crossed my mind, tears covered my face again. I don't know how long it took, but the dismissal bell finally rang. I imagined Golara at the water fountain, waiting for me so we could walk home together, and I knew for a fact that she would be the last student to leave school that day. I knew she was anxious too.

I started crying when I thought no one was at the school anymore. I felt so lonely. I was fine when I thought the other students and the teacher were there. But when everybody left, I was frightened to be alone in that dark, cold storage unit. I imagined my mama asking for me and Golara having no answer or explanation to tell her. I could imagine fear and concern in Golara's face. "I will be stuck here forever, and I can't get out anymore," I thought. "Perhaps these broken desks are the last things I will see." Grief and sadness spread through my whole body. I don't know how long I cried, but I cried to the point that I couldn't breathe normally. It felt like I was fainting. That much fear and anxiety was too much for a clueless first-grade kid. It was much worse than the night I got stuck in Bebe's yard.

The door opened finally, and I saw my mama and the school baba at the door. I was breathing shallowly, and I couldn't even talk when I saw my mama. She held me tightly and reassured me that everything was OK. She asked the school baba, "What happened? Why is she here?"

With a sense of remorse, he said, "You know I must follow the school's orders, or I lose my job. It looked like her older siblings wrote her homework, and her teacher was unhappy about it."

Mama knew everything about my new notebook and my home-work. Then School Baba said, "I made sure she was OK before I locked the door on her, and I promised I would come and get you, madam."

"You could have told her sister Golara to let me know," Mama pointed out, but he said he couldn't find Golara. Mama had come to school right after, but no one opened the door for her. There seemed to be a teacher conference after school, and School Baba was busy catering and helping. It was almost sunset, and I'd spent a day in that dark dungeon. I don't remember if I wet myself, and I don't blame myself if I did. I admit that I am still uncomfortable with darkness, even at this age!

I got my school bag and my notebook and went home with Mama. That notebook was not special to me anymore. As a matter of fact, I didn't like it anymore. As we were walking home, Mama said that the school was the reason she'd had to send our older siblings away. She was concerned seeing the school troubling Golara and me at such a young age. When I got home, I asked my mama for my old brownish, recycled-paper notebook. I never used that white notebook again, and I never wrote perfect homework, ever.

I waited too long to get that notebook. I only wrote on two pages of it, and I got punished for that neat homework. Today, forty years after that incident, I still don't like to write between lines or follow writing rules. I have good handwriting, but I choose not to use it. I still buy beautiful notebooks, but I never write in them. I just give them away as gifts. Perhaps someone else can use them without getting in trouble.

I skipped the next day of school, and Mama let me stay home. I don't know what happened at school, or what the principal told my classmates that made them avoid me when I returned the day after. They didn't want to sit next to me or even talk to me. They would start whispering and walking away when they saw me. But why? What had I done wrong? I did my best to respect everyone. I never got in trouble; I was a good student with good grades. I loved school and all my friends. Why did everything change after that day? Even Golara had no clue! She was lonely too. At recess, no one played with us or talked to us, and even our cousins who grew up with us avoided us. We were baffled.

My dream and vision of school were crushed. There must have been something else going on. My punishment was so cruel! I'd seen many trouble-making kids, even in my first-grade class, that were so out of control. They bothered and bullied other students, but they were never disciplined in front of other students, and they were never punished like I was. There must have been another reason that the principal chose to treat Golara and me in such a cruel and inhumane way.

8

WHY WERE WE NAJES?

On long fall evenings, Mama and most of her cousins got together at Uncle Amir's store. He was one of Mama's cousins, and they were stable, reliable relatives. Almost all of my mama's cousins lived in our neighborhood. After Uncle Amir closed his shop for the day, some of us gathered under a bright streetlamp in front of his store. Mothers and young girls chitchatted together and wove unique heavy-duty fabrics called *rouvar* using fine needles and cotton yarn. They would take the prepared *rouvars* to a shoemaker to make special shoes for men to use when climbing mountains or walking in the rocky fields. Children still ran and played around or did their homework together under that streetlamp. We wouldn't cause any inconvenience or disturbance to anyone, because almost all of the residents of that street were cousins, and the neighbors were perfectly OK with that gathering. It felt like we owned that part of the neighborhood.

One afternoon Mama sent me to buy some cooking oil from Uncle Amir. As I walked into his store, I saw Sedika, his ten-year-old daughter. She went to the same school we used to go to. When Sedika saw me at her baba's store, she called me a name, an unpleasant name, and wished me death. She then ran inside their house. I was shocked. Why was everyone acting this way? Uncle Amir, who heard his daughter's nasty name-calling, called her and asked, "Why did you cuss at your cousin like that?"

She replied with no pause, "Because she is *najes*, and it is a sin to talk to her or even look at her." Her father apologized to me and said he would talk to her later. He also sent Baba his best regards.

When I got home, I asked my mama while she was cooking, "What does *najes* mean, Mama?"

"It means unclean, contaminated, dirty, and untouchable."

"Why are we *najes*, then?"

She turned around quickly, looked at me, and asked, "Who told you that?"

I said, "Sedika!"

I saw a disappointed look in Mama's eyes. She looked directly at me and said, "We are not *najes* at all. Being clean and chaste is one of the rules we are required to practice."

"Why do they call us *najes*, then?"

"Because some people are not comfortable with who we are and what we believe. They label us to scare people away. They are afraid people will ask questions and convert to the Baha'i faith."

"Are we converting people?" I asked.

Mama answered, "No, it's every person's decision. We had this conversation before! I have to leave now!" She grabbed her *chador*, or veil, got the bottle of the oil, and went to talk to Uncle Amir.

It seemed everything went well at the store. Sedika was advised to apologize, and Mama came home with the cooking oil, but she was still offended. Although Sedika had promised her baba not to treat us that way anymore, things didn't go so smoothly at school. Sedika did not show any remorse there. As a matter of fact, she led a new group of fourth graders in bullying us at school. Those kids would follow us everywhere and make fun of us, calling us *sag-baa'bi*, meaning Baha'i dogs. They threw our books on the ground and pushed us around, and they laughed at us when we cried. All of this was happening under the eyes of that assistant principal, Mrs. Zamani. Even School Baba pretended he was too busy to notice, and perhaps he was busy, but I think he was more concerned about being labeled as Baha'i and, as a result, losing his job. He had no authority in the presence of Mrs. Zamani anyway.

It got to the point that I didn't want to go outside of my classroom anymore. The recess bell was like a nightmare for me. I would just go under my desk and hide until the recess time was over. Sometimes Golara managed to come to my class during recess, and we ate our snacks under my desk together. We didn't want to tell our mama about Sedika, because her baba was a good man, and we didn't want to cause any trouble between our mama and her cousins. But I didn't like school anymore!

Going home was another nightmare. The kids on the street would chase us and throw rocks at us. We just ran home and shut the door behind us. We didn't go out in our neighborhood, and our cousins wouldn't come to our house anymore.

We know now that a systematic brainwashing of children and young adults was taking place to prepare them for a greater movement, the Islamic Revolution. Those kids were allowed to practice whatever they'd been taught.

Karim was not going outside anymore either; he stayed home and made a large play farm with many clay farm animals. He formed them so perfectly. Baba built us a big brick dollhouse that we could fit in, and we loved it. Mama let us borrow some of her small dishes, and we played with them in our dollhouse. She also took time to teach us crochet and knitting. I still crochet and knit; it makes me go back to those days. I remember when Karim was sitting on the wall, watching the neighbor's children playing outside. He laughed with them and acted as if he was playing with them. I felt so sorry for him. He was like a bird trapped in a cage, watching other birds flying freely.

When we complained to our mama and told her how much we missed going outside, she said, "My children shouldn't be so weak and sensitive. All your older siblings went through almost the same trial during their school, and look at them now! They are grown-up, successful individuals."

It was heartbreaking to be reminded that Rahmat, our blind brother, was the one who'd gone through the most mistreatment and severest abuse and had still managed to stay strong. I am going to share only a portion of his difficulties later. Hearing those stories helped us to bear what we were going through, but why did we even have to endure all these troubles?

9

BEGINNING A ROUGH JOURNEY

I t was a late November night. Uncle Amir paid a surprise visit to our house. He sat down with our parents and whispered about what seemed to be some strange complications. He said, "You must leave the town as soon as possible. The clergy of the Friday Mosque gave a speech last night after the evening prayer. He was encouraging and inspiring those present to cleanse the town of all Baha'i families before Muharram. They needed to do that if they wanted Imam-Husayn to be satisfied with their deeds and accept their prayers. He said there should be no Baha'i living in the town."

We heard similar stories from multiple friends and neighbors who said that some people were planning to attack our homes. We were not ready to move out, but my parents sent Parvin and Karim to Shiraz a couple days later. Parvin was almost eighteen years old, a beautiful blue-eyed, tall, slender girl with long blond hair. There was a risk they could kidnap her. Karim was an energetic eleven-year-old boy. Mama was afraid he might get himself in a dispute with other kids, and that could lead to a conflict with parents. It would be safer if they sent him out of town to keep him and all of us safe. So that left only four of us at home, Mama, Baba, Golara, and I.

One night around nine o'clock, we gathered around the fireplace in the living room. Mama was reading us a story, and Baba was listening to his radio. We heard a knock at the front door, and Baba got up to answer it. He grabbed his handmade wooden spear in case he needed it. Baba was a man of the mountains and had a hair-raising voice when forced to face challenges. As soon as he opened the front door, we heard many young men shouting, cussing at him, and attacking him. We could hear his yelling grow more distant—it sounded like they'd surrounded him and were trying to take him away. We jumped in Mama's lap. She held our heads tightly to her chest and said, "Don't worry. Let's pray together. He will be fine." Then she started reciting, "Is there any remover of difficulty save God? Say praised be God! He is God! All are his servants, and all abide by his bidding." She chanted that prayer several times. I don't know how many times she repeated that prayer, but the mixture of Baba's yelling while under attack and our mother's whispered prayers in our ears caused a feeling that I can never explain or forget.

Fear and hope are very insufficient words to describe those moments. It was the battle of horror and courage, the clash of doubt and faith. I think Mama was praying in our ears on purpose so we couldn't hear Baba's last painful moaning before he was out of earshot. After almost twenty minutes, we didn't hear Baba's voice anymore. Mama got silent too. She held us tighter to her chest, looked at us, and said, "Be strong. They got Baba down, but don't be afraid. This is our test now, and we are ready for it." We started to cry about losing Baba, and we didn't know what Mama meant by our test. We had just had peaceful storytelling a few minutes ago; Baba had been relaxing in the corner of the room with us, with his radio on his chest. How could this wild nightmare have come to us so fast?

Mama kept us on her chest and continued praying, "Is there any remover of difficulty save God? Say praised be God! He is God! All are his servants, and all abide by his bidding." It was too frightening even to open our eyes.

The living room door opened a few minutes later. We felt a big shadow at the door. We were terrified of what would happen if they came for us. We were sure they had just killed Baba, and it was our turn now. Mama held us tighter and said, "Don't be afraid. Be brave. We are together."

Suddenly we heard Baba swearing. We just dared to open our eyes. He came inside and locked the door. Not a single scratch on him. He was panting and looked so mad and tired. He tossed his spear to a corner of the room and roared, "Not under my watch!"

Tears of joy ran down on our faces. We both ran to Baba, and each of us hugged one of his legs tightly. It was the best feeling to be his child at that moment. We couldn't stop crying.

"Are you hurt? How many of them?" Mama asked.

Baba replied, "Seven or eight little chickens with no guts or experience to fight." That was amazing! Baba was almost sixty-three years old, and he had just resisted many angry young men! They knew they couldn't take him down easily; that was why they'd attacked him in a group. He said, "I had to chase them all the way to the bazaar."

Mama asked if he knew any of them; Baba replied that they were all strangers, not a single person from our neighborhood. We had thought they were taking Baba by force and he was yelling because of pain, but it was the other way around—he was yelling and chasing them.

Baba said, "We will sleep on the rooftop from now on. Get everything ready. You have to sleep with your warm clothes and shoes on in case we have to escape from the roof. No noise or talking or lights! We don't want people to think we are home."

We got ready, putting on our warm clothes, scarves, and shoes, and went up to the roof. We slept on the roof silently, but anxious and frightened for the next couple weeks on the cold November nights.

Most of our immediate neighbors were Mama's cousins. We couldn't go to their houses, because it would have put their family at risk. Our grandparents who'd lived next door had moved to Shiraz since Agha-Hassan was sick; their house was not safe either, but we could still use their roof if we had to escape.

We didn't even go to school anymore. I kept practicing the same few lessons that I'd learned at school over and over. I remembered being so excited about going to the first grade, but I was not able to attend more than a few weeks. On a cold night, while I lay on the roof under the moonlight, I started shuffling through the passages of my books, looking at the pictures, and I asked myself, "Will I ever be able to read the rest of the pages of this book?" Just then a shooting star passed by!

Baba had started working on remodeling the house before these struggles began, and the construction was almost done. He had ordered a few pallets of bricks and instructed the deliverymen to drop the load inside the yard, but when the order arrived, they unloaded their trucks outside of the yard. Baba was home and repeated his request, but they didn't even pay attention to him or give any explanation as to why they were not following his directions. We were not sure if they'd left the bricks outside intentionally so they could have them handy when they attacked again, or if it was just coincidence. To be safe, Baba decided to carry the loads inside by hand. It took us the whole day to get those bricks inside the yard. It was a tense period, and we couldn't risk even something as simple as leaving a load of construction materials in the wrong place. Baba wasn't even thinking about finishing the house anymore. We went downstairs during the day, but there was no loud noise, no playing in the yard, no cooking, no guests, and no visiting anyone.

One early morning Mama's aunt, Ammeh Nessa', came to our house cautiously. She was a small eighty-seven-year-old with a hunchback, and walking and moving around was very difficult for her. She basically risked her safety coming to visit us. Like most of our Muslim relatives, she was a kind and caring person. She loved us dearly, and we loved her the same way. After a few minutes, when she was able to catch her breath, she told my mama that things were very complicated this time. Mullahs were inciting people to a big revolt and revolution. They were trying to convince people that Baha'is were spying for Western countries, and they needed to get rid of all spies to achieve freedom. They'd built a significant nationwide movement this time. You couldn't even defend yourself, and you knew they were running legal sources as well.

We didn't know what spies looked like or what their job was. How could they make such weird accusations about us—spying for Western countries? We didn't even speak any other dialect, let alone language. Aunt Nessa' said, "You know Muharram is coming soon. The clergy of Joma'h Mosque are talking more about Baha'is every night. As a matter of fact, they are planning to start with your house. They think if they get Mirza' Mohammad down, the rest of the families will be a piece of cake. I know I may not see you again—this might be our last conversation. But for your safety, please get out of town."

My parents had been planning to move to Shiraz sometime soon. They couldn't believe that, with the strong bonds they had made with people, some still were planning to betray them so harshly. Some people showed love and respect; some were just full of hate. That was so confusing, even to my parents. Aunt Nessa' kissed us goodbye and left with tears in her emerald eyes. She was right—that was our last conversation. We never saw her again.

10

ASHURA

Muharram is the first month of the Islamic calendar. It is the second-holiest month after Ramadan. The tenth day of Muharram is known as the Day of Ashura. It is part of the mourning of Muharram for Shia Muslims, and it's a day of fasting for Sunni Muslims. Shia Muslims mourn the martyrdom of Imam Husayn and his family in honor of their sacrifices. They avoid joyous events during Muharram. Shias begin mourning on the first night of Muharram and continue for ten nights. The commemoration climaxes on the tenth day of Muharram, known as the noon of Ashura, which is the most important day because it denotes the moment when Husayn and his family, including women, children, and elderly members, were killed.

The Shias believe Imam Husayn and his followers were deprived of water. The army of Yazid at the Battle of Karbala killed him and seventy-two of his followers. To commemorate Ashura, Shias practice different traditions, like hitting on their own shoulders with chains, beating on their chests to keep the rhythm of chanting for Husayn, and placing mud on their heads and faces. In some rare places, wounding themselves and their small children with knives is permitted as a ritual way to honor Imam Husayns young children. Although this practice is banned in Iran, some people still manage to perform it. These are some examples of the commemorating of Muharram that I witnessed for years.

It was the first day of Muharram. Four of us had been staying home soundlessly for the past few weeks, No playing outside, no communicating with neighbors and families, no talking out loud, not even cooking, because the smell of the food would give us away. I remember we had bread and plain yogurt that day. We were very careful not to make any noise. It was around noon when we heard a knock at the door. Baba got up to open the door, but Mama blocked him and said, "Not this time, Mohammad! They are not a few little chickens anymore. It's the beginning of Ashura, and they are coming from the mosque. They are all hyped and excited to kill you." Mama pushed him in the back room and locked him inside before he had a chance to discuss anything. Baba knew it was not a good time to argue with Mama. She told him, "Don't say anything. I will deal with them today." Baba was a strong man, but strength meant nothing when it came to dealing with Mama.

She went to the front yard to open the gate. At first it seemed only one person was knocking. No extra noise! But as soon as Mama said, "Who is there?" there was a second, then the third knock on the door. Within only a few seconds, you could hear so many men punching, striking, and shouting behind that door. Hundreds of small and big rocks started raining in the yard from the other side of the gate. Perhaps the reason our childhood game Raining Rocks has stuck in my mind for years is because it reminds me of that moment.

Those people walked so silently, no one could hear their footsteps. They wanted to catch Baba by surprise, without any warning. Mama didn't open the gate, and she kept her distance from the gate in case they climbed up the wall. We suddenly heard a loud cracking sound. That terrifying sound spread a strange feeling of horror and threat around us. That was the sound of a massive tombstone—they had taken it from the graveyard on their way to our home. They had planned to break the gate with that tombstone. And they did.

When they got inside the house, I saw at least two hundred angry men all in black, with chains, knives, stones, and spears in their hands. They started to shatter and destroy everything in their way:

windows, walls, clothes, toys, and dishes. They even crushed our little dollhouse and broke the small plates we played with. They got inside our room, where they tore books, rugs, and blankets and shattered dishes. I ran toward the bathroom at the other end of the yard. Those blasting pieces of stones came after me like comets. I tried to hide in a corner inside the shower, but when those big rocks hit the wall, the tiles shattered like sharp needles and sprayed everywhere. I don't know how long I was there; it seemed like those firing rocks would never end. I didn't feel safe anymore in the shower. Almost nothing was left to protect me. The mirrors, windows, and tiles were even more dangerous. I just secured myself in the corner of that small space one more time, held my breath, counted to three, and ran.

When I got outside, I witnessed a scene that I will never forget. In the middle of the yard, I saw my mother. Her face was covered in blood, and the blood came all the way to her neck and chest. Her clothes were torn, her headscarf had fallen to her shoulders, and her beautiful hair was messed up. I could see her bloody footprints on the ground. It seemed she was dragged around the yard, and her feet were bleeding.

I must stop at this point. Help me; oh heaven.

Whenever I face a challenge in life, that picture, the image of my mother, appears in my mind. That image has driven me to walk on the rough trails throughout life numerous times. It is a sacred image to me, and I don't want to forget it. But with regard to rough walking, what my mama had to go through on that day was the real walk on the edges of the blade; I just got to witness her doing it.

People couldn't stop their rage and madness anymore. They were at the point that they didn't even know how to stop. I saw Golara standing in the other corner of the yard watching. I couldn't move a step. I was shocked. I was not even able to cry. Mama looked at us, wiped her face, gathered all her strength, and with a glance asked us to come to her. Golara and I ran toward her and stood by her side, holding her dress. It was a brown dress with little light-blue or turquoise flowers on it. She grabbed us tightly with her bloody hands. She then called out to that angry, outrageous crowd with a powerful and determined voice I had never heard before. "Welcome to Karbala!" she shouted. That grabbed some of their attention. "Welcome to Ashura!"

She then continued, "Do you want to see what Karbala looked like? Do you want to grasp what Husayn and his family had to go through? You just created it today. Watch and mourn now! I am not any better than Zeynab, Husayns sister, and my two little children are not any better than Muslim-Ibn-Aquil's children." (The story of Zeynab and the children of Aquil is told during the ten days of Ashura.) They started to pay more attention now.

As she walked around the yard and looked at every one of them, she continued, "Now I understand Husayns loneliness, and I feel his estrangement. Now I see the pain his family had to go through. Thank you for making my home another Karbala today. Thank you for bringing Ashura to my house." Then with a powerful, sorrowful melody, she recited Imam Husayns famous last request, right before he got martyred. She said, "I call upon Husayn and his believers now. Is there anybody among you yearning to assist Husayn? Anyone who desires to come to Karbala and relieve him from burden and pain?"

Unbelievably, that angry, violent crowd started to wail with heavy grief and mourning, calling loudly upon Imam-Husayn. They shouted together, "Ya-Husayn!"

A call of shame and regret! They all dropped their weapons.

A heavy, deep silence spread around our house. No one said any word or made any movement after that speech. Everything looked like a flat picture—so motionless, so silent. It was a cloudy day, and it felt like we were looking at a gray-scale picture. Suddenly I felt a void, a vacuum that drew my mind from physical life. Those moments of silence were the longest thirty seconds of my life.

11

THIRTY SECONDS OF SILENCE

Those mysterious thirty seconds of silence were the turning point in my life. Had I not experienced those moments of pain, awe, and wonder, I cannot imagine which direction my life would have taken. Most of us discover or will experience such a sudden realization. It's not an object of teaching or a matter of learning. You as a parent may try to train your child to follow guidelines or teach them to perform rituals, but it's in everyone's very own life momentum that they discover their own truth. It is something very unique, like a spiritual birth. Those thirty seconds of silence were the beginning of my spiritual evolution. It was an awakening moment.

I couldn't feel my physical presence, I didn't hear anything, and my vision was broadened beyond this world. I could listen to my breath going peacefully through each cell of my body. It was a unique awareness of my true self, my soul. I could say I was able to sense the connection and yet the uniqueness of my spiritual and physical entities in those moments. I gained a general knowledge of the universe that lasted for an eternity of only thirty seconds.

That void, the empty space, that dignified silence: I found my identity at that moment. I knew who I was going to be, and I found the purpose of my creation right there. I aged in that thirty seconds; I was not a child anymore. I was very comfortable with my state of being. It felt like I'd been transferred to another dimension, and I was watching everything from a higher point. It was hard to comprehend, but I found that state like my permanent place—so peaceful, so sincere, and so secure. I'm not sure if it's a psychological trick your mind plays to save you from trauma, or if it's a real experience. But I could clearly see those people were not evil people. They were carrying out their pledge and vow to their beloved imam. They were not bad people at all; they were just led in the wrong direction, and I could forgive them easily, right away! It wasn't even worth being mad or upset. I learned in the matter of those few seconds that nothing in this world lasts, or even exists. This world was like a background or shadow of something else. I can't explain what it is. But those thirty seconds of silence changed me forever.

12

I GET KIDNAPPED

I was very comfortable standing next to my mama, holding her hand, knowing Baba was locked in a safe place. Most of all I felt blissful and proud. Suddenly someone grabbed me from behind, covered me with a large piece of cloth, and ran outside the house. Mama was shocked; she couldn't do anything. Perhaps she felt it was their new plan to force everything out of control again. I was frightened! Who could this person be? Where was he or she taking me? Everything happened so quickly. I was back in the physical world, and I felt that fear and uncertainty again. I heard someone chasing us. Whoever it was seemed to be guarding the house to make sure no one ran away.

"Where are you taking her?" he shouted.

"That's my daughter," said the person holding me. It sounded like a woman. "She was playing outside and ended up here. I am taking her home now. She has seen more than enough." I recognized the voice—it was our sweet neighbor Maryam. She was a good friend of Mama's and a loving woman who helped neighbors whenever they were in need. She covered her face with her chador and took me inside her house. She asked her husband, Haji, to keep an eye on me while she went back to get Golara.

Haji was a good friend of Baba's. A quiet and polite man, he didn't talk to me or even look at me. He poured himself a cup of tea and started drinking it while looking out the window. He was acting like everything was OK and there was no reason to be worried. I felt comfortable that I didn't have to explain what was going on at home. I sat at a corner of the room and waited for Golara to join me. I wasn't even crying. Maryam came after a while and said that she could not find Golara. I was sure Golara had been horrified as she watched me apparently getting kidnapped, and she'd run away. Later on we found out that she'd run to our lovely Aunt Kayhan's, who lived at the other end of the street.

Aunt Kayhan's twenty-year-old daughter, Shahin, opened the door for Golara but didn't let her in. She, like her siblings, clearly had a positive view of the revolution and had already started to treat us differently and unfairly. Perhaps she was afraid that, if those people chased Golara to their home, there was a chance they would attack their house too. Although she expressed her negative feelings toward us for being Baha'is, her concern about the safety of their home was a legitimate reason not to let Golara in. But I'm sure if Aunt Kayhan had opened the door, she wouldn't have refused Golara.

Golara started to run around the neighborhood, looking for someone to help her. Another good neighbor, Zahra, grabbed her and took her inside. After a couple of hours, when that crowd left and things seemed safe, Maryam and Zahra, who lived across from each other, took Golara and me back home.

When we got there, I saw Mama sitting in the middle of the room, crying. She thought she'd lost both of us. Her cousins were sitting around her, trying to clean her wounds and calm her down, but even they couldn't stop crying. Baba was sitting in a corner of the room, holding his spear and looking down, his expression deep and depressed. He said not one word; he was grieving quietly inside. He couldn't even blame Mama for locking him inside the back storage; Mama was not in the position to take any blame. The room was so crowded that our parents didn't realize our presence. Maryam and Zahra pushed us to Mama.

When our parents saw us safe and sound, they both held us so tight for a long time and cried with joy and gratitude. They thanked our incredible neighbors for risking their lives and saving us. They prayed and asked God to protect their children. I could see a sense of satisfaction and pleasure in Zahra's and Maryam's faces. May God bless them and their families as long as they may live. We had good neighbors and relatives, but our house was not a secure place for us to live anymore.

13

LEAVING HOME

Before Zahra and Maryam headed out, Zahra wanted to talk to our parents privately in the back room. She suggested there was a good chance that the mob would be incited again by the clerics and would come back again that night. Our house was not safe for us anymore. She suggested we go to her home using the neighbors' roofs. That way no one could see us or know where we were. Baba and Mama agreed and thanked her. We waited for everyone to leave our house. After sunset, when it got dark enough, we packed our documents and a few items of clothing and headed to Zahra's house using the roofs. Baba turned around to take a last look at our home before we left it. He had worked so hard to make a decent living for us and for his retirement. Now, at this age, he had to leave everything behind.

We got on the rooftop. The sky was clear now, and it was a full moon, so we could clearly see everything in the yard. This house was not the same house we'd woken up in that morning. Everything was shattered in pieces, broken and violated. Washed clothes were spread around the muddy yard, our little dollhouse was crushed, and our handmade dolls, Nadia and Anita, were stuck inside the dollhouse crying. Karim's bike was smashed and left in the corner of the yard. They had thrown it under a big blue truck and crushed it like a piece of junk. The front gate was twisted around that massive headstone like a piece of paper. Big and small dishes and pieces of appliances like the radio, TV, and stove were scattered all around. Our clay farm animals that we'd left on the trace to dry were crushed to dust. But worst of all—oh God, Mama's bloody footprints! The traces of her footprints were all over the ground. I could see how much pain she'd gone through to save her family. It was also so sad to see Baba in such a vulnerable position. He was always the one who helped others, protected others, and stood for justice, and now he needed help. I had never seen that much disappointment in his eyes. He took a deep breath and said, "That's OK. Thank you, God, for keeping my family safe!" He paused for a few moments and suddenly ran back downstairs. We didn't know what he was planning to do. We were supposed to leave quietly, so we didn't say anything. We just watched him from the roof.

He went directly to the barn, opened the door, and set all the animals free. It was so emotional to see him apologizing to those poor animals for leaving them behind. He took time to kiss and talk to each and every one of them, from Ghahraman, our gigantic white mule, to the little chicks, who were so puzzled to be awakened at that time of the night. He thanked them for their help and companionship. That was the moment when Baba broke down and started sobbing. He looked at the sky and said, "God! What is these poor animals' fault that they are punished so unfairly?" He then told them, "Hala'lam Konid"—forgive me. "I hope you find someone who loves you as much as we did."

I watched those moments behind a layer of tears when my innocent Pa-Pary and her little chicks walked outside the house, so confused and clueless about getting pushed out at that time of the night. I wished they could understand that Baba did it out of love. Baba then came upstairs, wiped tears off our faces, and told us not to worry. "They are good animals, and they will be safe. Our neighbors will find them and protect them."

We went from roof to roof to Zahra's house that night. There we heard that another mob had attacked one of our uncles' homes at the same time. To protect his family, he'd professed that he and his family were Muslims. I'm not sure if they beat him, but he didn't even dare to say a word against that mob. They took him to the mosque, and he professed to the clergy that he and his family were not Baha'i at all. It might seem that our uncle saved his house and his family, but we heard numerous stories throughout later years that he was forced to wear a shroud-shape costume to every gathering and walk that way in front of the crowd for their public ceremonies. Attending Friday prayers was mandatory for him, no excuses. Wearing a shroud was a symbol of sacrifice; it meant you had died to your old beliefs and were ready to sacrifice your life for the new cause you were supporting.

I am not sure if Baba would have been comfortable putting that shroud on and walking at the front in those gatherings. I am just glad he didn't have to go through that humiliation. My uncle's children had a rough time for the coming decades. They had to act like and prove that they were true Muslims, and even with all their efforts and actions, they were never safe.

On the same day, some neighbors went to another of our uncles, Ali, for help, but he said, "Bring Mohammad and all his children here and behead them in front of me. I never cared about him and his family." We are still not sure if this was his actual statement or just a rumor. We loved him dearly and always will. But unfortunately, that response at that critical moment was not surprising, especially considering some previous events between him and other brothers that supported this type of reaction from him. I heard some stories that he had been trying to get Baba in trouble since their childhood and throughout their adulthood. But Baba said, "I am sure he was not in a position to help that day. He had to protect his family too. I still love him and respect him. He is my younger brother." Baba indeed showed his love for Ali throughout his entire life. He never mentioned that day to Uncle Ali and never asked him about his statement. Bless his soul.

The neighbors also spoke with our youngest uncle, Rahim, who was seventeen years younger than Baba. He was only a small child when their father, Agha-Husayn, passed away. Uncle Rahim had great respect for Baba. Baba loved and protected him like his own son, and he was a father figure to Uncle Rahim.

I heard a story once that gave me an idea of how different my uncles could be. When Rahim was twelve years old, he went missing for a day. The family was looking for him everywhere. Someone found him suspended by one leg, hanging upside down in a deep well opening. Baba went to him and freed him. He asked Rahim, "Who did this to you?" Rahim's response was, "Kako-Ali," meaning brother Ali. A twenty-two-year-old man was trying to teach his twelve-year-old little brother a lesson. Baba was almost twenty-nine years old at the time and had to protect both of them. Since that incident, Baba had had to keep an eye on both of his brothers, for different reasons.

When Uncle Rahim heard about our conflict, he had a different reaction than Uncle Ali.

14

ESCAPING FROM THE TOWN

That night Aunt Nayera, Uncle Rahim's wife, paid an unexpected visit to us at Zahra's house. She told Mama, "You can't stay here for long. People will find you sooner or later and report you. I'll take you home tonight. We will hit the abandoned road outside the town. Rahim will send a pickup truck to get Mirza' Mohammad and the girls after midnight."

Uncle Rahim served in the civil branch of the army, the gendarmerie. His life was settled, and he had the most beautiful wife and five children. His wife, just like the rest of her family, was known for bravery and confidence. Her three brothers took a lot of significant risks through good and poor decisions. They didn't care what people thought about them. They were courageous, daring, and confident, and they made sure to use those qualities to protect others when needed. With their rough looks and brilliant hearts, they looked just like those Persian heroes in the book of *Shah-Nameh*.

Like the rest of our paternal relatives, Aunt Nayera was a committed and kindhearted Muslim. Mama told her, "Nayera! Do you know what you have signed up for? If people see you walking with me, they will kill you!"

Aunt Nayera pulled up both of her pant legs and pointed to two sharp bowie knives hidden in her socks. She then said, "I am not a true woman if I let anyone even get close to you. I swear to this holy day, and to my beloved Imam-Husayn, I will cut them in pieces."

Then she said, "Don't worry, I arranged a plan. My brothers followed me here; they are prepared. They will watch us from a distance on the way back home. You are not safe in this neighborhood."

Mama kissed us goodbye and left with Aunt Nayera. I will never forget that heroic action she and her brothers took that night for our family. And what Maryam and Zahra did, too, was such a daring risk.

We never saw those wonderful neighbors again to thank them. I am not sure whether Maryam and Zahra are still living or not. But I will never forget the good memories we had as neighbors and the great, selfless risks they took when we needed them the most. Aunt Nayera passed away five years ago, and Uncle Rahim passed away just few months ago. May they rest in everlasting joy together.

Walking some rough roads in life, I learned that people who have a broader vision of life tend to take more risks. When all your focus becomes surviving and protecting your possessions, the very direction of your life path can narrow to survival mode. But when you are not so concerned about your own well-being and interests, life opens more doors of opportunity for you. That's what Aunt Nayera and her brothers were about. This is a real lesson that I learned from experience at that young age. I have seen some people who were able to be helpful, but the fear of losing their possessions narrowed their path to the point where all they could do was guard their belongings. I believe that is another type of disability, but it's not visible. The fact that no one realizes how tightly those people get caught up in fear and weakness makes it even more difficult to understand. They believe they are judged based on what they have, not what they can do.

We had a long day, but even in the tense conditions of that night, before going to sleep, Baba still told us the story of the three naughty baby lambs, Shangul, Mangul, and Habbeh Angur, at Zahra's house. We fell asleep in his arms like other nights—so peaceful, so safe, as if nothing had happened to us.

Baba woke us up around two o'clock and said, "The truck is here. We need to leave." We were so tired, but we still managed to thank

Zahra and her husband for helping us. We hugged them and said farewell to them. That was our last visit.

Uncle Rahim sent one of his trusted friends to pick up three of us in a fruit truck. The driver hid us in the back of his truck behind empty fruit boxes. It wasn't safe for any of us to be seen in the cab. It was a cold December night, especially in the back of the truck. After twenty-five minutes of driving, he dropped us at Uncle Rahim's house. Mama was still awake, waiting for us.

We spent the next three days at Uncle Rahim's house, and they did their best to distract us from those troubled days we had just endured. Aunt Nayera was a large, funny woman. All of her five children had her features—tall, light skin, beautiful eyes fringed with the most adorable eyelashes, and a loud laugh. They made fun of almost everything. Aunt Nayera even wrestled with her son and won the competition. They made us laugh so much. They didn't leave us any space for worry in our days there.

Sometimes we could overhear Uncle Rahim and Baba talking. It was shocking to hear that, if Mama hadn't made that persuasive speech on the day of the attack at our home, and if she hadn't changed the mob's mind, we wouldn't be alive. Uncle Rahim had a lot of connections working at the gendarmerie, and he had done his research already. He asked Mama, "Did you see that blue truck?"

Mama replied, "Yes, but how did they fit so many people in that truck?"

Uncle Rahim laughed hard at Mama's simplicity. After a few moments of silence, he said gloomily, "They brought that truck and a long rope to tie Mohammad down and drag him around the town. They also had some petroleum in the back of that truck to set you on fire, Zivar Jan." He said if it weren't for what she had said, we wouldn't be sitting here together. I could see he was trying to hide his tears from us.

Uncle Rahim asked Baba, "Kako-Mohammad, do you know what happened to your animals that night?" He took a long, deep breath. "Some of those people who were still roaming around your house trapped them and set them on fire that night." I heard him say that they placed an old truck tire around our mule's neck and set him on fire, alive! They also threw the live chickens and baby lambs on the fire.

Uncle Rahim knew how much those animals meant to Baba; he was a man of nature, and he had a powerful connection with every creature. He loved them and treated them very kindly. Uncle Rahim continued, "I am not saying this to add more burden to your day. I am just saying this to give you a heads-up of how dangerous this area has become now. Clerics convinced people to avoid even your animals. I am so thankful that they didn't get to carry out their plan for you and Zivar, but you can't survive here, and you can't hide forever. You know I am not in a position to protect you anymore.

"This rage of Islamic Revolution is spreading everywhere, and no-where is safe anymore. You know most of the people who showed at your door were from my town, Bazaar, right?" He was right. None of our neighbors or relatives was among that outrageous mob. They were all strangers. I am sure they told the people of our town to at-tack other areas. It made sense to assign people from one town to attack a different town, because no one would attack their own rela-tives, neighbors, or friends. Rahim then said that he had arranged for another truck driver to take us to Shiraz soon.

Baba was actually happy to hear that. He told him, "You have done more than enough for my family, Kako-Rahim, and we are very grateful for your help."

Uncle Rahim told Baba about how the first truck driver he asked had refused to take us to Shiraz. The driver told Uncle Rahim, "Give me a cargo of opium and I will carry it easily, but a Baha'i family? Too dangerous these days." So Uncle Rahim had had to find another driv-er and offer him a generous tip to accept the task. Now he said, "The truck will pick you up a couple hours after midnight. You should pass the police checkpoint before sunrise. He will hide you and the girls behind his truck, and Zivar will sit next to him in the cab. If they ask him where he's going, he'll say he is taking his mother to Shiraz for medical treatment. Be careful not to attract any attention during this trip."

We had our last meal with Uncle Rahim and his family, and we left their house a few hours later on the truck. The driver arranged the truck bed so we could lie down. He put some thick blankets around us as safety cushions in case he had to take some unpaved roads away from the main road, or, if we had to escape, we would be safe and secured. He then set boxes of fruits around us on every side and secured them tightly so they wouldn't move. No one would guess we were lying down in the middle of those boxes unless we made noise. Baba held both of us girls in his arms on both sides and covered us with thick blankets, and we hit the road.

We used to watch the TV series *Little House on the Prairie*. I loved that show, and I had always wanted to ride a wagon like theirs. The thick denim fabric covering the back of the truck made me feel like I was riding in that wagon, and I felt so safe in Baba's arms.

I think the main reason that people can endure hardship and rough trails is their ability to see the bright side of the challenges and not focus only on the troubles. It was a tough journey, of course, but Baba still told us a story of a little cat that lost his most prized possession, his tail, and how he had to work hard to get it back from the old lady that took it. The story of that little cat caused me trouble twenty years later. Isn't that ridiculous? I will tell you about it in later chapters.

It was past midnight, and we fell asleep. I don't remember how we arrived at Shiraz, or if we went through any trouble. It was so cold in the back of the truck, and I pushed myself closer to Baba. Right before falling asleep, I tried to imagine our house one more time. I knew I would never see that house again. I tried to recall details of our home, our rooms, blankets and pillows, rugs, curtains, toys, school stuff, dishes, garden, neighbors, relatives, even our farm animals, especially our little chickens and innocent baby lambs that were thrown into the fire alive. I felt so sorry for our family and those poor animals. I don't remember when I stopped weeping before falling sleep.

Baba's arms were so warm and comforting. I was glad that they hadn't dragged him around the town with a truck and couldn't set Mama on fire. I was thankful for having them again. I couldn't even imagine what would have happened to Golara and me on that day if the angry mob had been able to carry out their mission. I was so grateful that we were in our father's arms once again.

15

ARRIVING AT SHIRAZ

We arrived at Shiraz early in the morning. We were happy join our older siblings and a few other relatives there. Sima and Reza rented a big house with multiple rooms together. My parents had sent Parvin and Karim to live with them a few weeks earlier. Sima had a two-year-old baby girl, and she was pregnant with her second child. It wasn't easy for Baba to stay in his son-in-law's home. It was a pride issue for a man like him. He never wanted to bother his two sons-in-laws and didn't want them to see him in a vulnerable position.

Mama's only brother, Uncle Behzad, and his family were a devout Muslim family who lived a few blocks from Sima and Reza. They had moved to Shiraz more than twenty years earlier, right after their marriage. Both of Behzad's parents, our grandparents, Agha-Hassan and Bebe-Golnaz, had become Baha'is many years ago, but they had to move to Shiraz when the first traces of revolution were rising. They were too old to face that much trouble back home. Besides the fact that they both were old, and Agha-Hassan was sick.

On the second day of our arrival, Mama and Baba went to visit Mama's parents at Uncle Behzad's house. Mama was recovering from her wounds, but she still felt obligated to visit her parents. Mama said that her father was very unhappy about Uncle Behzad attempting to take him to the mosque and make him convert to Islam. Uncle Behzad was not even aware that being a Baha'i meant accepting all manifestations of God, including the prophet Mohammad (may peace be upon him). Mama noted that Agha was very displeased. He said to Mama, "Please pray for me. I am walking on a narrow bridge of tests, like edges of blades, in the last days of my life."

The urge to join the revolution was taking place in all cities, and people started taking extreme actions in almost everything. Ideas or views like tolerating other beliefs, expressing your opinion, or even making a personal choice of clothing—ideas that had seemed reasonable only a few weeks earlier—were totally prohibited now. To keep his parents and family safe from those rebellious people, Uncle Behzad thought he would take his parents to the mosque so they could declare themselves to be Muslims to stay on the safe side.

His children were also under the impression that there was an urgent need for the revolution and removing the shah from power. To be honest, as a seven-year-old kid who had seen enough of the revolution, I didn't feel comfortable hearing anything about that word. My family had never been interested in supporting or denying anyone politically. We had just had enough! All we wanted was a safe place to live our life. But those young students were so excited about going to the streets and protesting. I am not sure how they feel now after forty years.

My parents went for a short visit that day, but they were advised to go to the mosque and free themselves from their troubles. Uncle Behzad told them if they declared themselves Muslims, they would get all sorts of financial benefits and support, like housing, a job, and insurance, in addition to the social safety. Baba told him he couldn't sacrifice his integrity and honor for money and benefits. He had lost all of his life savings and his properties. He had left behind his home, his family, and his people for his faith. It was unexpected for Uncle Behzad to make that recommendation, and it was strange for him to see Baba was not willing to tell even a little lie for the welfare of his family.

Uncle Behzad told them, "You don't need to change your inner beliefs. Just keep whatever you have in your heart and say you are

Muslim, but don't speak about your beliefs. You and your family will be free, and they will support you."

Mama responded, "Don't you think we could do that easily back home, without losing anything, if we wanted to? We left everything behind, we are standing up for our morality and beliefs, and we don't need to hide anything from anybody. We don't need any charity from mosques. We chose to stand up for what is right."

It seemed like a pointless conversation with Uncle Behzad. He eventually decided to take Agha to the mosque by himself, but that cleric was a man of honor. He asked Uncle how old his father was. When he heard almost eighty years old, he told Uncle not to bother him. He also advised his followers publicly several times to leave the Baha'is alone, as they were innocent people and there was no evidence showing they were involved with any political actions. Uncle Behzad stopped putting pressure on his parents then. One of the lessons I learned from that cleric was to realize that not all people from the same group are the same. You can always find good people anywhere!

16

RAHMAT GETS EXPELLED

A few days after our arrival at Shiraz, Uncle Behzad came for a short visit. He told Mama that he had received a phone call from Rahmat's school. They needed Mama to come. The city was under noticeable change. The movement of the revolution was getting stricter, and local government offices and schools were going on strikes. Everything was getting shut down, and Mama knew we needed to get Rahmat from school soon. She got ready quickly and headed out.

She was shocked to witness Rahmat's situation at the school. This is how Mama described her visit:

"It was a cold and rainy day, and I was leaning my head on the window of the bus toward the school. I was wondering how our next days would go. I recalled my last visit to Rahmat's school, when we attended his musical performance. Rahmat and his teacher took turns playing the tar and chanting poems on stage. I was so proud of my son, and I was happy to see his teachers were satisfied with his school performance, and how thankful he was about his school.

"I was so pleased to see he had the opportunity to learn and grow in an educational environment. I had a clear vision of a bright future for Rahmat, especially considering the fact that a few of his teachers were also blind. I dreamed my son would grow and achieve his goals, and I knew his disability wouldn't be that much of challenge for him in the future. I remembered how grateful I was at the last visit, and I considered how uncertain and nervous I was today.

"I was concerned that, if schools were shut down for some time, how was I going to take Rahmat home? We had no place to settle, and he couldn't run with the rest of the family. I was not sure how long it would take for schools to reopen again. I already had a hard time understanding our situation and planning for our next few days.

"It was still raining when I arrived at school, and it was their lunchtime. I went to the office, and they directed me to the cafeteria. I saw students sitting at their tables, enjoying their lunch and chitchatting, but I didn't see Rahmat among them. I asked about him. One of the people working at the cafeteria pointed to a door that opened toward the backyard. He told me that Rahmat was having his lunch there. I opened that door, and I found Rahmat sitting outside on a piece of a newspaper on the ground by himself while other kids were enjoying their lunch at the warm cafeteria. It was cold and still raining. I was devastated to see Rahmat sitting there on that cold, rainy day. He was shivering. The innocence on his face while he turned his face toward the sky made it look like he was still showing gratitude.

"Seeing him in that condition killed me inside. He looked like an abandoned child. My heart melted, feeling the oppression and injustice he was dealing with at that young age. Although my older children faced similar prejudice, seeing Rahmat in that situation was different. He was so innocent and wronged. I couldn't hold back my tears. He was a proud teenager, and I didn't want to make his day worse than what it was. I just wiped the tears from my face and walked to him and hugged him so tightly. I dried him with my chador. He was pleased by my presence, but I could tell that he had been through a few rough days. I blocked the rain with my chador and waited for him to finish his lunch. I still didn't want to disturb his meal. Then I asked him to go to his room and pack his stuff.

"I went directly to the office and asked Mr. E, the principal, why they were treating Rahmat that way. Had he done something wrong to deserve that punishment? Mr. E said very firmly, 'That's been his spot for days. Didn't you know about that? Rahmat has no complaints, and he seems to be pleased not to be forced to participate in his class activities. How come you are so upset?' He was trying to justify his action, and I was looking at him with disbelief.

"He then said, 'You know we had to prioritize our policies; we need to put our religious rules and regulations before anything else. I am sorry if that bothers you.'

"I asked him, 'What rule and policy tell you to put a blind child out on a cold, rainy day?'

"He replied, 'I don't need to explain it to you, madam. You know why he is sitting outside. You know we have had complaints from other parents that letting Rahmat sit next to other students will contaminate their food and eating place.'

"I told him, 'Mr. E! You have many years of education and service in your background. You are expected to know better and act better. Do you genuinely believe in that word *najes*?'

"He got upset, raised his voice, and said, 'Rahmat has too much confidence in himself. He keeps challenging us with questions, and if we let him continue, he will control the whole school very soon.'

"I asked him, 'Are you seriously scared of a fourteen-year-old blind boy?'

"He nodded and said, 'You know why we can't keep him here. I got his files ready, and I would appreciate you taking him home today. That is the reason we called you this morning.' So I picked him up and headed out, hoping to find a place to call home."

17

HEADING TO THE MOUNTAINS

I t was lunchtime, and we sat at the *sofreh*, a special Iranian fabric, which was spread on the floor and served as a table. We were so grateful to be together in that rough time. We were about to start eating when the landlord knocked at the door. She lived in the first room, close to the entrance door. She looked anxious, like she was dealing with an issue. She said some people had been watching her house for the past few days and had threatened her that, if those Baha'i tenants didn't move out, they would set the house on fire. She asked us to leave immediately for our safety and her protection.

It seemed Sima and Parvin hadn't had a chance to share their fears and concerns with us. They had been aware of alarming signs but couldn't say anything because we didn't have any other place to go. They had some threatening *shab-nameh*, night letters, thrown inside the house, demanding them to leave. The strikers banged on their door in the middle of the night and then walked away or used spray paint to write nasty messages on the walls.

That noon, the landlord looked so panicked and terrified. She advised us to leave immediately and come back later to get our belongings. We left the *sofreh* and our lunch as they were. We didn't even get a chance to touch our food. We never went back to get our belongings; our path was running in one direction, with no return.

That was the point that I felt we had become homeless. I can still sense how it felt walking with my family to nowhere on a cold, rainy day. I remember my sixty-three-year-old father, who once was a strong and proud man, with a worn-out coat and a dusty winter hat, holding some bags of pieces of bread, and my mama holding my blind fourteen-year-old brother's hand, trying not to walk too fast on those muddy, narrow paths. My seven-months-pregnant sister, Sima, has a hard time walking in the rain, and her husband holds her hand in one of his and a few bags of baby stuff with his other. I see my twenty-one-year-old brother, who worked a night shift at the hospital, deprived of sleep but still holding his baby niece tightly and trying to cover her with his Lee jacket so she won't get wet. I see my beautiful eighteen-year-old sister keeping her chador tight, trying to keep an eye on us younger ones. We have no direction, no clue or hope. I remember everything so clearly, like it was yesterday.

Our next option was our second sister, Nasim. She was married to a very kindhearted Muslim man, but Baba decided not to bother them for a few reasons. He was concerned that Nasim might be having a hard time at home, being under pressure to go to the mosque. In that case, it wouldn't be wise to put more pressure on her. We found later that she was safe and not under that pressure, luckily.

Reza suggested trying our last hope by going to our cousin Gholam, who'd grown up with my older siblings. He had moved to Shiraz a few years ago. Gholam was prorevolution and had engaged in a few related disputes with our mother before. He was not pleased to see us at his door. He was also concerned about the safety of his family, and that was a legitimate concern.

After trying our last chance, Baba said to us, "That's OK. We are the people of mountains. We can survive there better than in this strange city. We will find a safe place there, and we will come back to get our basic stuff."

Mama said, "Sima is only a few weeks away from having her baby, and her little daughter cannot survive this cold weather in the mountains."

We were walking to nowhere on that cold, rainy day, and the mountains seemed to be our last option. We agreed to head toward them.

On our way to the mountains, we encountered Sima's father-in-law walking to their house to visit. He had lost his home in Neyriz too, and he had been forced to move to Shiraz with his family right after we were. He was a good friend of Baba's from childhood. He said, "We came here two days ago, and one of our relatives has offered us a safe place that has already been under attack."

"How did you decide that house is safe?" asked Reza.

"It is in a military housing jurisdiction. The strikers didn't get to destroy it completely. They just got to shatter the windows. The house doesn't have electricity, water, or gas, but that's OK. A neighbor offered to run a temporary power line and a hose from their home. We managed to cover the windows with thick plastic and blankets."

Sima and her husband decided to go with him, and our parents were relieved that some of us had found a place to go. It was safer if we split into groups. The rest of us kept wandering with no clear destination in mind. Mama said, "I am not sure how my sisters are doing. Their houses might have been under attack too, but Tuba lives close. Let's go and see if they know a place we can go."

18

AUNT TUBA'S HOUSE

Aunt Tuba was pleased to see us, though she glanced up and down the street before letting us in. It was dark already, and we were soaked from the rain. We were so exhausted. Mama's other sister, Aunt Mehri, and her children were there too. Her house had been under attack also, and we had not known that. It looked like no place was safe anymore.

Despite all those challenges and hardships, we as children had quite a good time at Aunt Tuba's house during those few days. We were glad to see our cousins from our mother's side. They were somehow different from those on our father's side. It was easier to communicate with our cousins back home; they were easier to understand and more pleasant to talk to, and the games we played were different. My maternal cousins met us when we were in the most fragile and vulnerable situation, and that experience sometimes caused them confusion and even wrong judgments toward us, but we were able to overcome those issues as well.

One night before bedtime, we were having fun laughing and jumping on our mattresses. We didn't really want to sleep. Aunt Tuba asked us to keep quiet and go to sleep. Farid, who was almost my age, asked Aunt Tuba if he could show her a magic trick. She agreed on one condition: that we go to bed right after the trick. We all agreed.

Farid did a weird trick with his thumb so that it looked like he'd cut his own thumb off. Watching his trick, Aunt Tuba fainted and fell flat on the mattress. We got so scared to see her unconscious. We started to run around the house and anxiously called our mothers. They came to help, and shortly she was back to normal! I'm still not sure if she wanted to scare us or if she really fainted, but we always get a good laugh when we think about that night.

We had a good time at Aunt Tuba's while Mama and Baba were looking for different options to settle our family. Mama's youngest sister, Aunt Bahar, who lived in a different city, offered Mama their abandoned house in downtown Shiraz. They had no plans to live there, as her husband was serving in the military, and he was not sure where their next move would be. She suggested that we get the key from the previous tenant, who was another relative, and use that house temporarily. Mama got the key and took Rahmat with her to clean the house. She felt it would be safer if Rahmat accompanied her, as people wouldn't bother them as much. But she was surprised when she got there. This is how Mama described it:

"We got a taxi and headed out to that address. It was a small old house that needed some work. I saw the neighbor, a woman, standing on their roof like she was guarding the house. We opened the door and entered the front yard. She leaned forward and shouted, 'Are you the new tenant?'

"I smiled to greet her and said, 'Yes we are.' I was thinking perhaps she was trying to get to know us and welcome the new neighbor. But she yelled, 'Don't you even think of living here if you are Baha'i. I will burn this place to ashes if a Baha'i family moves in this neighborhood. We are cleansing this neighborhood from Baha'is.'

"I held Rahmat's hand and left immediately. We didn't even get a chance to check the rest of the house."

On another morning Uncle Behzad came to visit his three sisters. Baba was so exhausted and was leaning his head on the wall in the corner. He was trying to figure out our next move; we couldn't stay there forever. Uncle Behzad was mad at Baba for not listening to him and going to the mosque. He kicked at Baba's foot and shouted, "Get up! You are sleeping just like your fortune is sleeping."

Baba was at least twenty years older than he was, and he'd guarded and protected his family when Behzad was just a little child. He gave Uncle Behzad a long gaze and recited this line from a famous Persian poem from Sa'adi: "When God closes one door out of his will, he will open another door out of his mercy." But Uncle Behzad didn't let him to finish his words. He changed the poem to say, "When God closes one door out of his pleasure, he will put a stronger lock on it out of self-desire." He asked Baba again to confess and thereby free his family from its troubles.

Baba was so offended and upset. It was so hard for him to process the fact that he was in this circumstance in a strange place, with no money or support to move forward. And on top of all that, he had to deal with blame and accusations for losing his home.

Uncle Behzad was a good man with a kind heart, but it was hard for him to witness his sister going through so much hardship. His wife was a wonderful Muslim lady. She would cook a meal and cover it under her chador and bring it to us. It was not a short distance, and she would walk there every day. Uncle Bahzad showed a lot of respect and admiration in the later years when he understood why his sisters and their families stood firm for their faith.

Baba was so disappointed, and he left the house to find a solution. He was walking to nowhere. He didn't even have suitable clothing on, and he hadn't shaved his beard for days. We escaped from Neyriz in the middle of that cold night, carrying nothing. It seemed Baba had aged during the past few days. He was roaming around the town looking like a homeless man.

As I am writing this episode, I realize why that homeless-looking man, John, grabbed my attention at the summer youth camp! John and his story were significant to me because, in the back of my mind, I had the vivid memory of my father enduring those terribly depressing circumstances. Baba, a well-known, hardworking, and wealthy man, had become a homeless person. It explains why I still pay attention to any homeless person I see. I believe every person has a great story and dignity, regardless of their appearance or situation.

An old friend of our family's, Mr. Fazli, encountered Baba on the street. Sima's father-in-law had asked him to find us and check on our situation. He said he was on his way to Aunt Tuba's to get some news from us. Mr. Fazli said the Local Spiritual Aassembly of the Baha'is of Shiraz had evacuated the Baha'i center and converted it to a refugee camp. They still had a few rooms available, and he was willing to take us there. It sounded like a good plan, because Aunt Tuba's landlord had started questioning her, and her family was now at more risk. We moved out on the same day with the help of Mr. Fazli. We will never forget what Aunt Tuba and her husband did for us during those rough days when they were under so much pressure themselves. They were forced to leave that house a few weeks after.

19

BAHA'I CENTER, A LOCAL REFUGEE CAMP

A Baha'i center is a place for study circles, service projects, and volunteer work. Mr. Fazli knocked at the gate of the Baha'i center, and the large iron door opened. Baba was surprised to see that the person who opened the door was Mr. Lotfi, one of his childhood friends. Mr. Lotfi introduced himself to us children as the manager of the center. What a humble man he was.

The Baha'i center was an extensive rectangular orchard, with many rooms around the periphery and a lot of trees and flower beds in the middle. The trees were planted in two perfect rows through the terrace and to another gate that opened to the main street. Two beautiful flower gardens grew perfectly in the middle, with a man-made stream running between them. Mr. Lotfi said they had to close the main entrance on the other side for safety.

We noticed many families and children living there. That place was so quiet and peaceful; it looked like we had walked into another town. The people who resided there had diverse styles of clothing, and some spoke different dialects of Farsi, or even different languages. They were standing at their room entrances smiling and waving to greet us with joy. It was like a multicultural society, and I felt I belonged there. As Mr. Lotfi gave us a tour around the camp, we got to meet some of our new neighbors. You could clearly see in their eyes the same concern our parents had, the same passion and uncertainty. You could tell they all shared similar stories in their pasts. They had found refuge in that camp, just like we were about to find it. I hope one day they will tell their stories too. There will be thousands of books for others to read.

Mr. Lotfi guided us to our room. It was a small room suitable for about eight people if we slept on the floor. We were very grateful to have a place to ourselves. He then explained that it might be our room for now, but when the new families arrived, we might have to share our space. My parents agreed, as they knew more people would come.

It was funny to see we had nothing to put in that room. No rugs, no mattress or blankets, no dishes, no clothes. Nothing! We had only eight pairs of shoes in the corner and one small bag containing some of our legal documents. Nothing else! Yet that was the most comfortable moving experience we had. Mr. Lotfi mentioned that some Baha'is who were not affected by the strikers yet had donated a lot of household items and clothing. He then said he would let us take a break and give us a chance to meet our new neighbors, after which he would come and take us to the donation center to pick up items we needed.

We walked outside to see our neighbors. They were mostly our parents' age, from different cities of Fars or Bushehr. Bushehri people came mostly from Borazjan and Khormoj. They spoke Farsi with a thick southern accent. There were a lot of people from Fars province, cities like Neyriz, Abadeh, Daryoon, and even some suburban areas of Shiraz like Saedi and Marvdasht. I was amazed to see Baha'is from so many different cities.

Mr. Lotfi picked us up from our room and led us to the main auditorium. To the eyes of a seven-year-old kid, it looked like a large hall that could hold at least three hundred people. I am not sure how I would see it today. He invited us to take a cup of tea and relax there. They had removed all chairs and tables from the auditorium to create a bigger space, like a big family room for everybody to have breakfast together. Mr. Lotfi said, "You will be responsible for preparing your own lunch and dinner. The camp staff will provide the main ingredients for now. If you have local family members who can do grocery shopping for you, I recommend you have them do that." He then explained their budget was very tight, and they could not afford to prepare meals for so many families.

Baba said, "That is not a problem. My elder son Reza is working, and I will also provide for my family as soon as I find a job."

Mr. Lotfi said, "The next few months will be rough months. It's not a good time to look for a job. Baha'is are getting fired and losing their jobs everywhere. As a matter of fact, the whole city is on strike, and most of the shops, factories, and even government offices and schools are shut down." He then mentioned that they assigned different tasks to each family or individual to keep the camp organized. Baba and Mama agreed to help. I was concerned about not having enough food to eat.

We went to another big room where they kept donated items. I call that room the donation room, but they had to change it to another purpose later on. There were many used items, like dishes, carpets, and a lot of clothes and shoes of all sizes. Some dry foods, like bags of rice and grains, cooking oil, and bread were donated by the families who hadn't been attacked by the strikers yet. Like the rest of my family, I was not happy to accept charity, but we had to take a few items for now. We got a couple of blankets and pillows, but we were tired, so Mama said she would go back to get some stuff the next day. I guess she didn't want to take used items when Baba was present. There were some individual-size tubes of toothpaste, toothbrushes, small shampoo bottles, and one towel for each of us; we took one of each item. Honestly, brushing my teeth every night had not been a concern before coming to Shiraz, but we developed the habit when we moved to the Baha'i center. It was because the neighboring children would call each other and walk as a group to the end of the garden where the bathrooms were. We would play and laugh and even scare each other in the dark. We still managed to have fun.

Mr. Lotfi said, "Breakfast time is at 7:30 a.m., and if you want to attend the dawn prayers before breakfast, 6:30 a.m. is a good time." We thanked him, and he left. We were so grateful for the new place and our new neighbors. I felt content knowing that we didn't have to face the trouble alone anymore and to see so many families and children from different cities living the same story, knowing we could help and protect each other as a big team.

The next morning we were so excited to go to the main hall for breakfast. They had set three long rows of tablecloths down as *sofreh* on the floor to create more space for people to sit. First we chanted some prayers together. I felt the energy, and it was so uplifting and inspiring to be a part of that group, living through the same history and standing up for the same cause.

One of the members of the Baha'i center management welcomed us and talked briefly about the history of the faith in its earliest stage. He reminded us about the times when the groundbreakers of the faith had to walk the same path we were on. He encouraged everyone to be patient and stay strong, to have faith. He said that if we wanted to carry the message of peace and unity, we should walk some rough roads, and we should stand up for what is right. We should be assured that our devotion and contributions would pay off, and our county would be free of ignorance and bigotry toward any minority. As he was talking, I remembered the day our home was under attack, and how my mama was able to transform them and focus their awareness in the right direction. I believe the speaker was right; he told us to forgive them, as their intention was to serve their faith, but they had been misled and misinformed. Because most of us were from Muslim backgrounds, I would say he was right.

The center was incredibly beautiful and serene, and the people who lived there were simple, friendly, and courteous. It seemed like we had known each other for years. We all knew that this would be a temporary stage for us, and we would go in a different direction soon. We might never see each other again, and we appreciated every moment of this journey together.

Public schools were still shut down. Therefore a home-based school was arranged for the children residing at the center. An adequate section of the center was dedicated to serve as a temporary school. That little school had a library, a few study rooms, and an outdoor field for basketball, volleyball, and a playground. At night when everyone gathered in the auditorium, students participated in some activities that were prepared for the day. Interacting with those children was most pleasant. No one judged another person's accent or looks. I didn't have to crawl under my desk during the break anymore. I was glad that Golara could sit next to me. There were not enough rooms for each grade, so they combined some classes. The material taught in those classes was not an official public school curriculum but a more general study designed to keep us busy, and we all had to share books. Our teachers were so thoughtful, friendly, pleasant, and sometimes funny. They lived at the center too, and they were walking the same journey as we were. We got to experience some peaceful days there, but we knew it was temporary.

In the second week of our stay at the center, Sima, her husband, and their entire family arrived. They couldn't survive in the broken house. The neighbor who had offered to help couldn't continue supporting them anymore. We were so glad that Sima and her children could live with us at the center, but there was no other room available at the center to settle them in. They were a part of our family, and it was the best for all of us to stay in one room. We had almost twenty-four people living in that tiny room. At night women and children slept inside, and the men rested outside at the terrace. More people took refuge at the center, and most of the rooms had almost the same number of people as we did. In spite of all the hardship and difficulties we were going through, we had the most joyful time together.

Another lesson I learned at that young age was that your happiness is not tied to your wealth and belongings; it's mostly related to your perception of life and your commitment to righteousness. That sense of awareness, the bond of fellowship, the power of sacrifice, the thought of detachment, and most of all the power of love and unity grew us stronger as a community. Our parents were honored and grateful to have been chosen to walk on that path and to be a part of the history that will illuminate the way for future generations, rather than suffering in a rich but miserable life.

The strikers found out that the Baha'i center sheltered many families, and they wanted that it to be evacuated soon. Their unofficial organization, called the Revolutionary Guard, started invading the center unannounced to disturb and threaten the families who lived there.

20

A BIRTH AND A DEATH

One January morning when we were at the playground, Mama called us in and told us our grandpa Agha-Hassan had come for a short visit. Agha-Hassan and Bebe-Golnaz, our lovely grandparents, were our next-door neighbors back in Neyriz. I remember he called Golara and me *naneh-koochika*, little moms, and we liked that nickname. I felt so special to be called that name, because I knew Agha-Hassan had lost his mother at his birth. There were visible scars on his face; Mama said he got them in different incidents when he was a child. I always felt if Agha had had his mother around, he probably wouldn't have had those scars. I am sure he also bore a lot of invisible scars inside. Just like his sweet sister, Aunt Nessa', who came to visit us and advised us to leave Neyriz, Agha had the most innocent smile and bright emerald eyes. He loved us all dearly, but I could tell I was one of his favorite grandbabies. I loved him so much and couldn't imagine my life without him.

I remember when we went to their house, I would directly go to him and sit on his lap. He hugged me and patted my hair, told stories, sang songs, and showered me with love. I recall a day when he helped me climb up and hang from a large pomegranate tree in their yard. He told me if I wanted to get tall, stretching exercises and hanging would get me there. Whenever I got a chance, I kept climbing, hanging, and swinging, just like a monkey.

Years later when I joined the volleyball team at high school, I wished Agha were around to see me. I thought of him at each volleyball practice. By the time I was fifteen, I was taller than all my sisters.

Agha-Hassan was a tradesman, and he traveled to different cities and brought us cute little pendants and pretty ornaments. He also brought us *masqati*, a soft and sweet treat from the southern part of Iran. I still think of him and all the good memories we had with him whenever I have some *masqati*. Agha-Hassan and Bebe-Golnaz had to move to Shiraz because he became ill a few months earlier.

Mama called us in from the playground, and we ran to our room to see Agha-Hassan. I wanted to give him the biggest hug and sit on his lap again. We had missed him for so long. I used to see him every day back home, but I had seen him and Bebe only once for a short time for the past few months. I was surprised when I saw him. He looked so weak and had lost a lot of weight. He sat in a wheelchair outside our room, covered with a blue blanket, with an IV connected to his arm. His eyes were closed, and his head was down. He was quiet.

He opened his eyes and smiled, then said, "*Naneh-koochika!*" I was glad he still remembered that nickname. I couldn't believe his illness had progressed so severely in a matter of only a few weeks. I felt so sad to see him in that condition.

Golara and I knelt down in front of him and held his hands. We rested our heads on his lap and started crying speechlessly. Golara and I could always communicate by eye contact without saying a word. We grieved losing him as an active playmate and our beloved grandfather. It seemed Agha felt it too; he patted our hair, gathered his strength, and said almost in a whisper, "Don't worry, *naneh-koochika*, everything will be OK soon. I am going on a long trip. What do you want me to bring for you?"

"When are you coming back, Agha?" I asked.

"Soon, inshallah. Everything will be fine, and I will be OK." We all knew that was our last visit, but hearing those words of hope from him gave us comfort.

Uncle Behzad had taken Agha to the hospital, but they were not able to admit him to the operating room. The Revolutionary Guard were present everywhere, including the hospitals, to make sure the wounded protesters had first priority for treatment. They accepted other patients too if they swore an oath against the shah. Agha was not in a position to answer that question or to wish anybody ill in the last days of his life. It was a strange and cruel demand to force upon someone at such a weak point in life. They left Agha on the floor of the hospital and denied him treatment. The hospital, like every-where else, was under martial law, and they wanted him to confess a belief in Islam before going for surgery. Agha was facing a final test in his last moments. He had fought so many battles during his life, but he believed this was his ultimate test. He didn't want to lose that battle and fail his faith.

It was impossible to take Agha home; three of his daughters had lost their homes, including Aunt Tuba now. The fourth daughter lived in another city. We understood why Uncle Behzad couldn't take Agha with him. He was concerned if Agha passed away at his home, their neighbors and friends would come to offer condolences, and he didn't feel safe or comfortable taking them to the Baha'i cemetery. He didn't want his neighbors to know his parents were not Muslims. That sounded reasonable from his point of view, and his sisters didn't want to put pressure on him.

Uncle Behzad had no choice but to bring Agha-Hassan to our room. He explained about the conditions in the city, including the hospitals. It was getting worse; everything was so out of control. No hospital would accept Agha, and he didn't know what else to do. Ehsan, one of the volunteers who frequently visited people in the camp, mentioned he knew a doctor in Isfahan. Ehsan also was an ex-cellent protector for Rahmat in those insane days; he was one of the few people who understood Rahmat. I remember on one of the last days of our stay at the Baha'i center, when it was under threat, Ehsan carried Rahmat on his back to make sure he was not left behind. I will never forget that scene. Ehsan was arrested and executed a couple of years later in a Shiraz prison, and his death had a significant impact on Rahmat. I will tell you about it later.

The trip to Isfahan was an eight-hour drive, and Agha would not be able to sit that long. A friend had a car, and Reza was a nurse. Bebe-Golnaz and Reza got on the road to Isfahan with him on the same day. None of Agha's four daughters were able to go with them. They were all on the run, protecting their families and children.

Mr. Farhad, a good family friend, and his family welcomed Agha and Bebe to their home in Isfahan. Agha was too weak to receive any treatment. He passed away two days after his arrival. He didn't cause any trouble for his family. They stayed for a few more days to bury his body in Isfahan; we were never able to visit his grave. This is a chance for me to thank Mr. Farhad and his family for making sure that Agha's final days on this earth were peaceful.

Back at the camp, Sima was in the last days of her pregnancy. Mama was grieving the loss of her father while so much was still going on there. Sima started to have pain. I felt sorry for Mama. She was under so much pressure but never complained about anything. Sometimes I think no one could take as much pain, stress, and responsibility as my mama did. She was grieving silently for her father, and now her daughter was having labor pains. Sima's husband, Reza, and Mama took Sima to the hospital.

The Revolutionary Guard had prosecuted Sima's gynecologist as well as many other Baha'is who served in critical positions. He was not able to work; he probably was on the run. They had to take Sima to a state hospital. Sima said that they admitted her, but all the doctors had gone on a general strike. Only a few nurses were working, and they were obligated to ask if a patient was prorevolution in order to treat them. Sima had to go for a C-section, as with her first birth. No doctor was willing to perform the C-section on her. She and her baby were at risk of being in their last moments. Mama started running around the hospital, crying and pleading for someone to have the heart to help her daughter. One doctor came and ordered her vital signs to be taken. Her blood pressure was too high, and the baby was struggling for his life. At that point they took Sima to the operating room.

Death and life can be joyous moments under normal circumstances. We want them to be special, peaceful, memorable, and unique. But when the gates of life open, whether one is arriving or leaving, things can get totally out of hand. Sima had planned for her second birth to be special, just like the first one, but she was struggling for her life and her baby's life, while she was under pressure to renounce what she believed to get treatment. Nothing was normal in those wild days. It felt like we were living a never-ending nightmare.

Sima gave birth, and she and her baby boy were OK despite all the issues they had to go through. They got another chance to live. They were released from the hospital in a few days; it was ten days after Agha's passing. That baby brought a lot of hope and joy to us in those frightening days.

21

TRAUMATIC SHOCK

The Revolutionary Guard would show up at the gates of the Baha'i center unannounced at any time and demand to inspect the camp. Sometimes rebellion strikers climbed the walls in the middle of the night to disturb the camp and the people who lived there. They would break branches off the trees or stomp on the flower gardens as a reminder that the camp was under their watch and control. During the day they would come inside the Baha'i center, walk around, and disturb the families, demanding they leave. The management of the Baha'i center asked families to send their young daughters to safe places outside the center if possible, places like relatives' homes. They asked the young men to guard the camp walls at night. They also appointed a few reliable, experienced men to stay close to the entrance gate. The purpose of having them at the gate was so that when the intruders showed up, those considerate, courteous men could have a civilized conversation with them about our situation and reassure them that the families who were sheltered at the Baha'i center meant no harm to anyone. They hopefully would convince the trespassers to leave without causing any problems.

I remember the day when Eskandar, one of the young men stationed at the gate, tried to speak simply to them, and they asked him to step outside the Baha'i center to talk. They then seized him and took him to an unknown place. When he came back the next day, he had a large knife wound reaching from his right shoulder to the left side of his back. They had beaten him severely and made another large cut under his left eye. He was able to get himself to the hospital and get his wounds stitched. The hospital probably admitted him because many people showed up at the clinics with similar injuries in those days.

Most of the young girls were placed in different locations outside the camp; our parents sent Parvin to stay with Nasim and her husband. The Baha'i center was under intense observation, and it wasn't safe to have people from outside visiting us. Things were getting more complicated with each passing day. The city was under siege, and we were stuck inside that refugee camp. The more intense and severe the outside environment got, the more pressure was forced upon us inside those walls. And we as youngsters endured it.

One morning I was sitting alone inside our room. I wasn't feeling well that day, and I had a slight fever. I had just learned to draw a little princess with curly hair and a puffy dress. Tara, a fifth-grade girl who lived in the next room, had taught me to draw, and I had been trying for days to get it perfect. Forty years later, about two weeks ago, I encountered Tara at a gathering at the Northern Virginia Baha'i Center. What an amazing coincidence! She is a fifty-year-old woman now, but we remembered each other very well. I even asked if she remembered the picture of the princess she taught me to draw. She didn't, but I have reason to remember that princess drawing clearly. That sketch got stuck in my mind, and I still draw it sometimes in its very same childish way.

Back on the day, when I was sitting in that small room practicing my drawing, I felt a large shadow at the door. I thought it was Baba or one of the men who stayed in our room. Sometimes, during the day, they would stop by to pick up some clothes from their bags. So it wasn't surprising to see someone coming inside the room; that's why I didn't even look up to see who the person whose presence I felt. I was leaning over my notebook on the floor, practicing my drawing.

Suddenly I felt the man direct a hard kick toward me, almost hitting my face. The pages of my notebook and my colored pencils scattered everywhere in the room. I looked up with a shock. There was a stranger, a huge man with a full dark beard and mustache, with his thick eyebrows drawn together. He wore a forest-green uniform and a pair of heavy army boots. He had a rifle, and he looked so furious even without it. I felt so afraid just looking at him. He shouted, "Get up and get lost!" Then he cussed at my mother. I was scared to death. In those quick, shocking moments, I had a flashback to the day our home was attacked. I was thinking maybe this time they would kill everyone, and I probably would be the last person to die. Then I heard a whizzing noise in my ear, and I passed out. I can't remember the rest of that incident, but I heard later that on that day, they had entered the Baha'i center by force and threatened everyone, trying to intimidate us into leaving.

I opened my eyes and found I was lying in Mama's lap. I was shivering, and I couldn't talk. One day passed and I still couldn't speak, I had no appetite, and I was still shaking. I wasn't even able to cry. Mama and Baba were talking about how pale my skin had turned and that it didn't look normal. Reza and Mama took me to the emergency room. They admitted me because I was a child, I guess. Mama and Reza sat at my side. Mama was crying silently, and Reza was holding my hand. He started to sing me my favorite song, the song that he used to sing when he came to visit us at Singing Willows:

> *Khahar-e naz-e koochulu*
> *Digeh natarsi az lulu*
> *Oh my darling little sister*
> *Don't be afraid of the monster*
> *Your brother will sit by your side*
> *And he will sing you a lullaby*
> *Don't close your eyes because of fear*
> *Laugh, sister, again; laugh, I am here*
> *Let's borrow a pair of butterfly wings*
> *Fly to the mountains where angels sing*
> *Let's borrow wings and fly free*
> *Up to the lands of joy and glee.*

I remembered the old days when Reza would visit Singing Willows and sing that song for me, and I would laugh and scream on that huge swing set. It was so joyful and amusing. But that day I wanted to cry to get the ache out of my chest. I was so tired, and I felt a lot of pressure on my throat and in my chest, and I couldn't even cry. It seemed that much fear was too much for a kid like me to handle. I don't know the medical terminology for the diagnosis, but I think the doctors said it was traumatic shock.

In addition to the traumatic shock, my throat and neck started swelling. I was bruised on the sides of my neck, and that hurt so much. They said that I had also developed mumps, a viral infection that affected my salivary glands and throat. That was the reason I had a fever that day. They kept me in the hospital for a week for both conditions. They prescribed me some antibiotics and advised my parents to keep me quarantined in a separate room.

There was no place in the camp to use for that purpose, but since I was a health hazard, they decided to empty the donation room and put couple of beds in it. They also evacuated the small storage room next to it to use as a little clinic. Reza and a couple of other people at the camp who had experience in the medical field volunteered to help with running the clinic.

Because my illness was contagious, Mama got sick too. She had to stay in that isolated room with me. I felt so bad that Golara and Karim were not able to see Mama for days. Mama got sick because of me, and I am sure everybody in our family needed her. A couple of days passed, and they brought another patient in.

22

LIFE AND DEATH IN THE QUARANTINE ROOM

The new patient was an elderly woman, and she wasn't in good shape. They didn't reveal her identity to us, and Mama knew it was for her protection, so she didn't ask her name. The elderly lady seemed to have delusions and kept talking in her sleep; you couldn't tell if she was asleep or awake because she kept praying and crying. She was so restless. I am not sure if she had faced traumatic shock too, or if it was just a matter of her age and condition. Perhaps hospitals refused to give her care too, or there was another reason, like safety, that they couldn't take her to the hospital. It looked like she was passing her last days. I believe she had had a stroke, but I'm not sure about that. She looked like a well-known and wealthy woman, and I am sure she had some people or family to take care of her, but it seemed no one was able to access her in those unsettled and tense days. Perhaps her children were running away, trying to save their own lives too. Nurses would come and check on her and give her medicine and, if possible, some food. But she refused to eat. She was so impatient and restless.

We didn't know her children, and she would not communicate with anybody. It seemed she was in another dimension. A few days passed by. Three of us were stuck in that room; no one visited, and we couldn't leave. I remember standing at the window, watching other kids playing in the yard. It was like the days when Karim was watching other kids playing outside and he couldn't join them. But there was a big difference between Karim and me: I didn't want to go out anymore. I was so tired of dealing with trauma and tension. I had lost interest in everything.

I thought I would always be an energetic, happy, and curious girl. I would ask questions and discover the world. My dream was to one day become a teacher or serve in the army. I remember when young military girls came to our town as teachers or nurses. They were called Sepah-e-Danesh, meaning the Army of Knowledge. Their muscular bodies, their beauty, and their army uniforms always impressed me. They were tall and robust, with long braided hair. I had always wanted to be one of them when I grew up. But I couldn't imagine my future beyond that dark, isolated room and that camp. Nothing could make me happy anymore.

One day when I was at the window, watching the kids play, I realized the old lady was not talking or mourning anymore. It seemed that she had fallen asleep silently. I saw Mama covering her with a blanket. I asked Mama, "What happened to her?"

"Nothing," she replied. "She is just tired. She needs to take a nap now." Mama stepped outside the room for a moment. That was my chance to see the old lady's face. She was beautiful. I was glad she had finally reached a point where she could stop being so restless. She was sleeping so peacefully, as if she had received pleasant news. Her face looked like she had never had any concern, pain, or worry.

Mama stayed quiet at her bed and said a little prayer in her heart. She then sat next to me at the window and tried to point out some objects and the different children playing outside. Later I assumed she was trying to distract me when nurses carried the old woman's body out of the room in a blue-and-white blanket.

We learned the reason they hadn't revealed the woman's identity was to protect her and her son. I still keep it confidential to respect and honor to her wish. Her son was a well-known and honorable colonel with many years of service to his country and his people. He and many Baha'i scholars from different fields were persecuted during and after the revolution. He was arrested and executed with many Baha'i professionals a couple of years later in Shiraz. When he was in prison, he wrote to his children about his life and the fact that he had lost his mother at a young age, and that a loving, caring stepmom, the lady who had passed away right next to me, had raised him as her own son. He described that lady as a very knowledgeable and faithful woman. I am sure his family has a great story to write about his life and his sacrifices, if they haven't done so yet.

23

MOVING OUT OF THE BAHA'I CENTER

Mama and I spent almost two weeks in the quarantine room before we were finally allowed to leave it, but things were not much different outside that room. Families felt more and more pressure and fear each passing day. As things got more troubled outside on the streets, there was more pressure on us to leave the Baha'i center. Behind those tall walls, we could hear gunshots, flames roaring, cars burning, protesters yelling, and people screaming. It was a disaster outside. It felt like nothing was stable out there.

While we were grateful that we were not homeless and were shielded inside the Baha'i center, we also felt we were being forced to move out as quickly as possible. The Revolutionary Guard wanted to confiscate the center, and they would come inside any time; they didn't even have to use force. They were armed, and they followed no rules. We were not in a position nor had the capacity to stand up to them. That wouldn't have been wise, and we were not there to fight. Although no one was safe, and many Baha'is were running for their lives, I didn't believe they would kill all of us on the spot, as there were a few hundred of us living there, all families with children. They just wanted us out. That's why they disconnected the electricity, water, and gas lines, knowing we couldn't survive for too long.

Humans are fascinating creatures. They perform a mourning ritual for Imam-Husayn for his being banned from accessing water on the Day of Ashura fourteen hundred years ago, and yet they cut the water supply for many families with young children and elderly members as a service to God.

We couldn't survive anymore, and it was not safe for the families to stay there any longer. The Baha'i center management decided to send families to different safe places. Some people whose houses were not under attack yet, or some kindhearted Muslim friends, offered to give the persecuted people like us a safe place to stay. Most of the families were out by the third day of power disconnection based on their makeup, like the age of their children or the number of elderly people.

Our family stayed another week to find a place. We were one of the last few families to move out. They relocated us together with three other families in a house in the central part of the town. We moved out with a little white truck, and we had only a few items to take with us.

24

GETTING BACK TO SCHOOL

It was January 16, 1979, when the shah of Iran left the country. That was the day when the protesters celebrated their big victory. They came out on the streets once more, but this time to celebrate and cheer their success. The military had already surrendered its power to the revolutionists and joined the protesters. People were dancing in the middle of the roads and congratulating each other. They offered sweets and flowers, and cars played loud, joyful music and honked their horns. We had no idea what would happen after that, and neither did the demonstrators who had spent months fighting on the streets. Although they didn't seem to know where the change would take them, we hoped that day would be the last day of their aggression and fighting. Schools opened a few days later, and everything was expected to go back to its normal routine.

Mama registered us at an elementary school. It was a long walk there. Baba walked Golara and I to school and waited there until classes were dismissed. He still wasn't sure if he could leave us at school, since he felt things were not yet safe. He stayed in case another problem arose and we had to leave school. Shiraz was a new and unfamiliar city for us, even before all the changes. He didn't feel comfortable leaving us at school. It's not easy to imagine your father waiting five hours for your school to dismiss, then walking you back home. That simple act of sacrifice by Baba showed us that school was in fact essential, and we had to take it seriously.

We were able to catch up quickly with our grades, but things had gone in a completely new direction in the matter of a few months. The teachers had to wear hijabs, and female students had to cover their heads with a new style of black scarf called a *maghna'e*. We also had to wear a newly designed long, loose dress and pants as our school uniform.

No one knew us in that school, but we still were cautious about our limits and making friends or making conversation about different subjects. We carried this concern through the end of high school. The morning programs started with reciting the Quran, and the new national anthem was added in later months. At one point they played and sang the first revolution song, which was performed by a famous actor named Reza Rooygari, every morning. That song was to honor their supremacy and victory. To be honest, children never liked that melody; it sounded too harsh, and it was frightening for us. Mama took Rahmat back to school too, but they didn't accept him.

We lived in that house with the other two families for another couple of months, and we got along very well. Things were settling down on the streets. No protesting, no fire setting, no Molotov cocktail throwing. February 1, 1979, was the day on which the revolution took its final step with the arrival from France, the supreme leader of the Islamic Revolution. We were following the news, and we hoped people had finally found peace and acceptance, and that the end of their rage and hate was at hand. No visible harassment or persecution was going on. For a while, it felt safe to move on with life in that new city.

94

25

MOVING TO AN APARTMENT

We had no plan and no place in mind when we left the house, and we didn't know where our next step would take us. We knew that we had to move out of the house, since it seemed safe now, and the owner of the house had been so kind as to let us stay safe there for three months. One of Mama's sisters, Aunt Mehri, mentioned there was a new type of house, a few of which were available for sale at discounted prices. I am not sure why those houses were sold at a discount; perhaps the owner of that project had had to abandon it or leave the country. To my young mind, the poem that Baba had recited to Uncle Behzad on that cold, rainy day applied very well: "When God closes one door out of his will, he will open another door out of his grace."

Aunt Mehri said the new type of little house was called an apartment. It was the first time we'd heard that word, and it sounded very strange to us. We had grown up in a substantial, sizable farmhouse, with lots of space to run around and trees to climb, and we could fly to the meadows and mountains where the space and sky were our only limits. Aunt Mehri explained that these little houses were small, blocked, and built on top of each other. We had always seen neighbors residing next to each other, not on top of each other. It sounded funny to us as kids. We had another memorable reenacting of the two neighbors living on top of each other, and we had a good laugh after months of fear and distress. Even the word apartment alone sounded so cramped and tight to us. But Mama, Baba, and Reza agreed to go and see them.

As much as Baba was a hardworking man, Mama had always been a wise and foresighted prudent wife. She always kept some money for rainy days. My eldest brother, Reza, in spite of all the financial burdens he had on his shoulders, had been able to save some money too, and Sima's husband also offered to lend us some money. They put all the funds together and bought an apartment. We moved a couple of weeks later into a two-bedroom apartment on the fourth floor of the building.

Mama was so happy that our apartment was on the fourth floor. Her logic was that if we had to face the same trials again, no one could climb the walls or throw stones that high. She was also very thankful that our house had been attacked during the day rather than at night. We still get a good laugh when thinking about her reasoning. I don't yet know how to explain her being so faithful and prepared for any test at any time. Perhaps she and Baba got used to the perpetual harassment and mistreatment to the point that they were grateful to have different options on their menu of tests. They could always predict and prepare for the worst. That was a bitter truth.

Back home Baba had been about to retire, but he had to start all over at his age in an unfamiliar city. He found a job as a security guard for a big construction company. It was a double-shift, on-site job, which meant Baba had to live there. He could come home once a week. The management had built him a basic temporary room of concrete blocks right outside the building. Baba lived there for two years—two cold winters and two hot summers. We missed him so much at home, especially Golara and I, who used to sleep by his side and listen to his stories before our bedtime. Sometimes not seeing Baba would get so unbearable that they took us to him for a short stay. That concrete room looked more like a solitary cell than a room; it could fit only a small bed and had a tiny space for a little stove. Baba kept a small teapot and a few dishes in a box. Seeing Baba, a man of the mountain, who had lived his entire life freely, being trapped in that tiny room to earn a little money broke our hearts. It was like seeing a lion in a cage.

I remember the day after our first visit. Golara was so disappointed and hurt to see Baba in that situation. When we got home, she refused to eat for days, to the point that she became paralyzed. She kept crying and asking to get Baba out of that place. When Baba came home on Friday, as he usually did, he reminded her that was the only job he could find for so long. He was not in a position to quit, but he told Golara if she really wanted to help him out, she could start eating again.

As the youngest child observing everything, I learned to be self-sufficient and to require as little time and work from others as possible. I learned that sometimes, not doing anything or saying anything was the best thing I could do to help. When the construction project was over, Baba was sixty-six years old and looked much older than his age.

Our life in the apartment was quite different. We had to be very careful about making noise. I can certainly say we never got to play freely like we used to. Walking, playing, singing, or even talking was always a concern. That lifestyle might not be unusual to a child who is born and grows up in an apartment, especially nowadays, when so many indoor activities are available for children that they don't even want to engage in any outdoor games. But for us, living in a small apartment was like living in a crate.

We didn't know any of our neighbors, and we didn't even feel comfortable making any friends at that point. I think one of the reasons the three of us have better art skills is that we had to practice many quiet activities and crafts at home. As I mentioned at the beginning of this book, I asked Karim to paint a view of Singing Willows, and his work is shown on the cover of this book. I am sure he remembers more details of that meadow than I do.

Karim got a new bicycle, and Golara and I took turns riding with him, since the bike was too big for us. We decided to take it on the roof to play, carrying it down sixty-eight steps was fun only for the first few days. The houses in Iran have flat roofs, and the roofs have curbs and borders around them, so it was safe for us to play up there. We also created a seesaw on our roof using leftover lumber and concrete blocks, and the asphalt covering the roof created a big chalkboard for us to draw and write on. We played a lot of hopscotch games there too. Soon that roof became our very own playground, and it was a clear example of the phrase "Necessity is the mother of the invention." Later, many of our new friends and new neighbors' kids joined us in playing there.

26

SCHOOL IN SHIRAZ

There was an elementary school across from our apartment, so close that we could see children playing in the schoolyard from our balcony. My first grade had already been messed up; I went to school for only a couple months in Neyriz and a few weeks in Shiraz. I can't recall many good memories of the first grade. The second grade, however, was better. The school was close to our home; I could see our apartment from the classroom window. I was very excited about my new school and making new friends, especially Maryam.

Maryam was a very polite, kind, smart, and sweet girl. She was the best student in our classroom. Her grades and her manner and behavior were so unique and novel. I felt very comfortable around her, and I was so glad that she'd picked me to be her best friend too. We were always together, and with her help, I was able to catch up with school very quickly. Her father was a high school teacher, and she could ask for his help if we needed assistance.

Maryam and I spent a lot of time together, and I learned so much from her. With her presence, the new city and the new school didn't feel so strange, and I built more confidence in my fresh start. She had a very delicate spirit and a soft voice. I remember a song she taught me, and I really enjoyed singing it with her during our break time. I still love that song, and I sang it to my children numerous times many years later. My children loved it too.

Yek Shab-e Mahtab
Mah miyad to A'b

The glow of the moonlight
Will pass through the twilight
It will drop in the bay
And it will take me away
From Sahara to Sahara
And valley to valley
It will take me to a meadow
To that green chanting willow
A little fairy by grace
Tiptoes in the place
She walks in with care
And combs her soft hair
That green willow tree
Keeps dancing with glee
And stretching its arms to the sky
To those little shining stars
One little star then drips
And swings down and sleeps
I know one of these nights
The glow of the moonlight
Will drop in the bay
And it will take me away
From Sahara to Sahara
And valley to valley
To that serene meadow
By that singing willow!
Where I walk by grace
And tiptoe in the place
I will walk with care

And I'll comb my soft hair!

As I am writing these lines right now, I realize something unique and remarkable: that song is describing a place just like my home, Singing Willows. In that stage of my life, when I was struggling to process the unpleasant events I had gone through and to understand the things I had seen as a child, when I was trying to adjust and push through my daily struggles, that particular song from my kindhearted friend Maryam helped me to push through and see the bright side of life. Isn't it amazing? It is amazing to see how nature, the higher power, God, or whatever you call that source of comfort and confidence sends you solace and relief when you need it the most, and sometimes, like in my case, you don't even realize it until some forty years later. That's amazing. His love and grace for us have no time and place, and if angels exist, Maryam was one of them for sure.

At the end of the annual grading period, my teacher, Mrs. Ghodsi, told me that she had good news for me: Maryam had earned first place in our class, and I had earned second. I was so happy for both of us, and I was grateful to have met Maryam, who helped to change my direction in the right way in school. Mrs. Ghodsi asked me to be prepared, because they would call and reward me the next day at the morning lineup. I realized that I had equal opportunity now, and I could forget about first grade and reach or even exceed my school expectations.

I was so excited when I got home. I told Mama, "Guess what? I earned second place in our class, and I will get rewarded in the morning lineup tomorrow."

Mama was so excited. "*Afarin,* my darling baby!" she said ("bravo"). "I knew you could do that!" That achievement could be the end of my challenges at school. Kids would know me and treat me even better now, and I would be back on my school track again. I woke up early the next day and got ready. I was so excited about school.

The morning program started. After daily routine programs, they began calling students to reward them. They started with the fifth graders. It took forever for them to get to the second graders.

Maryam and I held each other's hands and were so excited that we would be called soon. Finally they called Maryam's name. I squeezed her hand and let her go with a smile and excitement. She walked in front of the line and got on the stage. The principal, Mrs. Ghodsi, and other teachers were lined up there. They shook her hand and gave her a certificate of achievement, plus a gift box. I was so excited for her, and I was applauding and screaming with such joy, and I knew I was the next one. Maryam stood on the stage next to other students, waiting for me to get called and stand beside her. My heart was beating so fast. I didn't know how to handle that much excitement and joy. I wished the principal of my old school who'd thrown me in the storage shed for writing good homework could have been there to see me standing before everyone, shining with confidence again.

The assistant principal grabbed another folder; I knew it was mine. She got behind the microphone; I closed my eyes and listened impatiently. An incredible moment was about to come. The principal announced, "And the second place for math, science, and Farsi goes to...Leila Sadri."

I don't need to waste another paragraph about how it felt when they didn't announce my name even as the third or fourth place. Mrs. Ghodsi explained to me later that the board of review had found some problems qualifying me, and they didn't think I was eligible to receive second or even third place. She didn't say anything about my work or my achievements. I was the problem—I did not get qualified.

As a Baha'i student, I got to hear that statement, "Not qualified," numerous times during my school years, and I got used to it. Another time when in eighth grade, I won a poetry contest. My literature teacher told me in advance that I would get the award, but again, the board of review didn't qualify me. My poem was OK, but I was not qualified to get the award. Or when in high school, I pulled myself up to varsity volleyball, and our team went to play for the state championship. We practiced and played outside from 6:00 a.m. to 3:00 p.m. every day during that hot summer. Yet in the end they didn't qualify me to travel with the entire team. There are many other examples.

I grew up hearing that statement of not being qualified applied to almost every achievement I truly earned at school.

One of my goals and dreams when I entered the United States was to finish school. But each time everything was headed in the right direction and I was close to achieving my goal, I just quit. It was so frustrating after pushing myself to withdraw intentionally. I asked my mentor once, "Why do I keep doing this to myself?"

She enabled me to dig the answer from my past and myself. It was because, on many occasions since my childhood and during my lifetime, I had been treated unfairly and even punished for the achievements I earned, whether it was clean, excellent homework, playing varsity volleyball, or participating in school competitions. Even writing a children's book about a little cat got me in trouble in later years. My mentor explained that whenever I was close to reaching my goals, my subconscious chose to stop me taking the last step. It was a hidden method to protect myself from getting hurt and disappointed. To be honest, I am not even sure if finishing this book is a good idea. I am not sure how I will handle the outcome of that.

27

THE STORY OF THAT CAT

The story of the little cat was always in the back of my mind. Baba had told us that story when we were escaping from Neyriz as we lay on the back of a truck, fleeing for our lives on a cold November night. Many years later, when my son was six years old, I wrote a rhyming children's book of that story. I illustrated all the characters and presented my work to a publisher. Mr. Rezaei, the owner of the publishing company, accepted my book, but he said to be able to publish the work, we needed the final approval from the Ministry of Culture and Islamic Guidance.

I received a phone call from Mr. Rezaei in few weeks. He wanted to see me. He said it was a matter that he preferred to address in person rather than on the phone. I was very excited about that meeting. I got my six-year-old son ready and headed out to their office. I wanted my son to see if he put efforts and work toward his goals, he could achieve them. But things did not go as I expected. Mr. Rezaei handed me a letter from the Ministry of Culture and Islamic Guidance. He said my book had been rejected, and he advised me not to follow up or even ask for another answer. He suggested it was a warning for my safety, and it would be wise just to drop everything at that point. I couldn't believe I had gotten in trouble for that simple kids' story.

I will tell you briefly the story of that little cat, in case you are curious. It is rhythmic storytelling in a folkloric style, and it has fast, repeated lines that get really challenging as the story moves forward.

There was an old lady who lived in a teeny tiny house by her-self. She had a simple, clean home. She would wake up every morning and do her daily routines. One morning a little hun-gry cat got into her room and drank from a glass of fresh milk, which the old lady had set aside for her breakfast. To scare the cat away, the old woman threw one of her slippers at the cat. Unfortunately, the glass of milk broke, and the cat's tail got twisted as it ran away. The cat was so upset and started complaining. He asked the old lady to fix his tail, or his friend would make fun of him. The old lady told him, "I am sorry for your twisted tail, but you can get it fixed when you bring a cup of milk back to me."

Here is the brief sequence of the story. In every scene, the repeti-tive, rhythmic, fast conversation between the cat and other characters makes the story distinctive.

The cat goes to a goat; the goat says she is hungry and needs some hay. The cat goes to a farmer to get the hay, but the farm-er says his shovel is broken. So the cat goes to the ironsmith to get a shovel, but the smith says he needs to eat first. The cat goes to a chicken to borrow an egg, but the chicken says she can't lay until she eats some grain. The cat goes to the market, where a storeowner says if he really needs some grain, he needs to help around the store and earn a cup of grain as his wage. So the cat agrees to work in the store for a day.

The story goes in a backward sequence then, visiting all the charac-ters again. Telling this story leaves you breathless, and it encourages hard work and trying to earn your way.

Mr. Rezaei said the ministry believed my book was intentional-ly written to brainwash children and the younger generation. I was shocked to hear that statement. "Why?" I asked.

He replied, "They believe the cat in your story represents the geographic shape of Iran, the broken glass of milk is our revolution, and you are trying to say all our hard work and efforts for the revolution were wasted."

I couldn't believe they were able to come up with such a strange accusation. I don't think you can bear to hear about the further consequences that a few people and I had to experience because of that children's' book. The punishment for that story was so cruel. I will probably take that part of my journey to my grave and present it to the higher authority!

28

FINANCIAL STRUGGLES

B ack to the story. It had been a few months since we moved
to the apartment. Everything was moving toward normality.
Then one morning Reza came home after a long night shift,
and he seemed anxious and concerned, but he didn't want to talk.
We thought he was tired or had a rough night. We left for school,
and he took a nap. In the afternoon, when we came home, Reza and
Mama were conversing about finding Reza a new job. Reza had been
the primary breadwinner of the household for the past few months
before Baba had started working. We didn't ask anything about the
issue, but it seemed something serious was going on. We sometimes
overheard the conversation when the adults got together. We had to
be cooperative and understanding and not ask many questions. We
knew yet another issue was on the way.

The same night, Nasim and her husband came for a visit. Nasim
worked in a different hospital. It looked like she was dealing with
some troubles too. We were very nervous. I thought they had found
out about us living here, and we were about to face another attack.
I was already tired of running and hiding. I had been dealing with
some disturbing images in my young mind for a while. I thought if
they were so creative as to lay out a plan to drag Baba around the
town with a truck and to set Mama on fire, they had a more acces-
sible option to kill us here. They could simply throw us down from
our fourth-floor balcony. No neighbor knew our story to help us. No

one cared to take Golara and me to save us. I could even imagine my classroom window across from our apartment being the last thing I would see as I fell to the ground. My hopes and dreams of going to school were just a foolish fantasy, I thought. I would never get to grow up and live like an average person. Perhaps I didn't even deserve to grow up like a normal kid.

We sat quietly around the room to see what was going on. Why were Reza and Nasim so distressed? Nasim said there was a federal mandate from the new Islamic government to lay off all Baha'is from employment positions. The only condition by which they could keep their job was to publicly declare they were Muslim in a local newspaper.

Looking back on all those years living in Iran, I don't think converting from the Baha'i faith was an option for people like us. I have seen many people who lost their homes, their jobs, their loved ones; they were imprisoned, sentenced to death, and had to leave the country, but very few refused to abandon what they felt to be the truth. One who did was my uncle, and I am sure he deeply regrets that decision. He had to make extra effort to prove himself Muslim, and even still, his children never lived a safe and peaceful life.

A new radical movement was taking place nationwide, and it was based on one viewpoint: to separate believers (*moe'men*) from infidels (*kaafar*). These terms served one purpose: to sift the infidels from the nation. Anyone who was not aligned with the ideology of the Islamic Revolution would be removed. It drew a clear line between adherents and those who were considered to be misled, and in their view, Baha'is were the most deceived group. Therefore people who got laid off because of being Baha'i were not able to find employment again. Reza and Nasim had both lost their jobs in the matter of one day.

Nasim decided to stay at home, since her husband was working and they had no children, so her not working was not that much of a financial burden on them. Later on, though, Nasim had to start helping relatives and neighbors who required simple medical care. She even started to crochet and sew to make and save money, and soon after, she bought an electric knitting machine. She got so busy very quickly with her new home-based business, in addition to her medical services. She spent most of her money helping the ones who were struggling financially, and her husband was a kindhearted Muslim man who supported all her work and effort to take care of others. Reza was not able to find a job, so he started selling small items like socks, hats, and small toys on street corners.

Back home in Neyriz, we didn't have financial struggles. Baba was making good money, and most of our daily needs were covered. We, the last three children, were the only ones living with our parents. Now we had lost everything, and our older siblings had moved back to live with the family. Baba was already working, and the money Reza was making was not enough, and it wasn't fair to put the entire burden on him.

Rahmat, was expelled from school, and no other facility would accept him. He was so desperate to help the family, but there was no job opportunity for a person with a disability, and he had too much pride to ask for help. One day when everyone had left the house and it was quiet, he grabbed his tar, went to a corner, and chanted prayers with such a beseeching and imploring voice. I had never heard him reciting in that tone. I had not even seen anyone play the tar so intensely, giving the instrument such a strange, unique sound. It didn't sound like a tar at all. I don't know how he played it. He didn't think I was home, and I didn't want to disturb his peaceful practice. For many years I listened to his music and quiet singing, and it touched my heart every time. Rahmat became a significant part of my life later on and remains so even today.

With the financial struggles the family was going through, almost everyone started to work, and Rahmat was no exception. Reza helped him to start his own little business selling goods on the street corner. They would go together so Reza could keep an eye on Rahmat's items. Karim, who was thirteen, started to work for a small painting company. I could tell he was not comfortable working there, but he didn't say anything to our parents. We as kids could see Karim was anxious and unhappy with his job, but he didn't want to add more stress to our parents' plate. We started to crochet small items like hats and washcloths for Reza and Rahmat to sell. When I look back and think about that period of our lives, I can say I am so proud of my family. We never gave up on each other, and everyone played their part to keep the family together. This was Mama's phrase: "When a load of difficulties falls down, it's everyone's job to put their shoulder under it and do their share." And that's what we did as a family. That's how we lived for the next few years.

29

AN ARREST

One summer morning, when Reza and Rahmat sat under the shade of a tall building selling small goods, a bunch of flyers was dropped from the top of the building. One of the flyers floated down close to Reza. He was curious to see what it was about, so he picked it up. It seemed it was a poster announcing an antirevolution party, encouraging people to join them, to fight the revolution and the new changes. This is how Reza described that incident:

"Within less than ten minutes, many armed Revolutionary Guards rushed onto the streets. They started to attack and arrest anyone who had those flyers in hand, and I was one of them. They put handcuffs and blindfolds on us and pushed us into army vans. They took us to an unknown place.

"They were cursing and beating us on the way. When we got there, they let us out of the vans but didn't remove our blindfolds and handcuffs. We spent the rest of the day being interrogated, insulted, and beaten. They didn't even let us sit down or stand straight. After many long hours of questioning and investigation, they detained a few of the people they'd arrested, but they decided to let me go, since I was just selling stuff at the street corner with Rahmat, and they were convinced that I'd had nothing to do with distributing those pamphlets. They walked me out of the interrogation room, removed my blindfold and handcuffs, and ordered me to leave.

"I was in shock and disbelief when they removed my blindfold! I opened my eyes, and I saw myself inside the Baha'i center. The place that had sheltered and protected us for months was now under their control and had been turned to a detention center. I felt so much pressure and ache in my heart to see they had turned that holy place into a prison. Two security guards were escorting me out of the center, and it wasn't wise to show any emotion at those moments. I didn't want them to know anything about my past, as it would raise more questions, and they might keep me there if they suspected anything. I acted like I was there for the first time. I went through such rough moments seeing the spirit of peace and love locked in prison, seeing the shelter for families to take refuge not so long ago now changed to a jail.

"As they walked me out of the main gate and I passed by each room, I remembered every family who had lived there. Many friendships were shaped there, and I recalled all the good memories we had in that rough time together, all the tears and laughter, hope and fears. As I passed the auditorium, I could even recall many of us chanting prayers in a group. For us that place was the spot where our past and future united—a past with so many strange stories to tell, and a future with so much uncertainty and hope to come.

"I remembered all of that, and I knew I had to be smart and strong, or I would be in trouble again. It's hard when you are experiencing so much emotion and pain, but you have to act like you don't care. It's hard to ignore that much pain and disappointment."

Learning to live a normal life with all those fears, concerns, and challenges, settling down to our new lifestyle, was so complicated, especially when our never-ending trail kept branching off into random paths and directions.

30

THE WAR!

T he Islamic Revolution was moving toward its final phases of implementation. A vast elimination and execution of previous officeholders had already taken place at the higher levels of government. Most of the parties who had contributed to the success of the revolution were now labeled as foreign opponents. The country was dealing with massive domestic changes and challenges. The new government was being shaped into a unified Islamic party, with no competing parties permitted, and there were many layers of uncertainty for those living under its rule.

In the middle of all these changes, a bloody war started between Iran and Iraq. The two neighboring countries had experienced disputes for many years, and several military incidents and diplomatic conflicts had occurred in the past, but there had never been an actual war.

The war started in the fall of 1979. Iran had spent most of its resources and energy on domestic challenges; new workforce members were selected and appointed based merely on their commitment to the revolution's goals rather than their expertise, experience, or knowledge of operation. That governing void created a perfect opportunity for Iraq to put military pressure on Iran. I will not go through details on the cause of the war, for that's not my expertise, but as a person who lived most of her youth during those terrible years of fear, desperation, pain, and horror, I must tell how that war affected our country, our community, and even our families.

I can clearly recall those sad days when we observed the "martyrdom" of young men who volunteered to go to the battlefields, young soldiers whose remains were later delivered to each town. Each neighborhood had lost at least a few young men. We all felt, as one nation, the pain, the grief, and the loss of those young men. The names of streets and roads were changed to the names of those young men who once had lived there; those streets, roads, and highways still bear their names. Some families lost multiple sons, brothers, and even older men. Thousands of young adults signed up to fight the war, and they were accepted unconditionally.

I remember when trucks were driving through the neighborhoods to collect items like blankets, first aid supplies, food, money, and any other materials we could offer. Our home economics projects switched to little financial support efforts for the battlefield. We sold our cooking, sewing, and knitting projects to collect money, and we sent it to our brothers and sisters who were fighting at the borders. Those were years when the whole nation worked together to support our troops in defending our country. Don't get me wrong; I am not advocating the idea of war in any manner, nor were most of the people who were dealing with it at the time. People were still trying to process and comprehend the outcomes of the revolution, and the war caught them completely off guard. No one wants war to ruin their country and kill innocent people, and no one was ready for it. All we could do was protect our land and our people.

It still was not safe for people to know we were Baha'is. The oppression and the violence against us as a minority were still going on. There were and still are people who think their job is to eliminate us from the earth. In spite of the hatred and violence against us, we Baha'is always helped our people and our country. There was no time or need to mention anything that might cause more conflict when our country was under attack.

The war lasted for eight years; I was eight years old when it started. Living on the fourth floor of the apartment during the war was not the best experience anyone could have. I remember "the red alarm" or "attack alarm" frequently going off. Every radio and TV station, mosque, school, and local office would play that frightening alarm at the loudest volume. The electricity, gas, and water services would be suspended. We were not supposed to use any type of light like a flashlight or even candles. We had to seal the windows with thick, dark curtains. We walked quietly down our long, dark stairways. The alarm would go off multiple times some nights, and we had to be prepared to run at any time. We had to have our shoes and clothes handy in case we had to run for shelter, although nowhere was completely safe.

I remember the few times when Shiraz was under attack. The sounds of those explosions are the scariest sounds I can remember. They said the blast waves of the explosions were more damaging than the blasts themselves, because they would affect a person's brain and nervous system. If an explosion happened nearby, people could lose their hearing and eyesight, or the dense blast waves could damage their brains, resulting in mental problems for the rest of their lives. There are still a lot of people dealing with the permanent damages of waves.

During the terrifying hours of a long attack, in the pitch dark, when you couldn't see anywhere or anything, little children would be crying, and adults would be whispering nervously, guessing what part of the city was more at risk. That was a frightening blend of voices. You could feel that almost everyone was shaking and shivering. In those eight years, during the day or night, we had to be prepared for the worst. We took shelter, but we knew nowhere was safe until the red alarm was cleared.

In addition to the red alarm, there was a yellow alarm to warn that Iraqi aircraft had crossed our borders. We needed to stay alert to their flight to determine whether they were coming to our skies or changing their direction to a different target. Shiraz was a significant

Iraqi target because of its petroleum refinery. The white alarm meant the end of the attack emergency, and we were safe to go back to our normal activities. Most homeowners had dug deep tunnels in their yards in which they could take shelter; they believed those tunnels would protect them from the explosion blast waves.

Almost every young Baha'i male who reached the age of military service performed his mandatory two years in the Iranian Army during that war. Many Baha'i soldiers lost their lives, were disabled, or went missing on the battlefield. But when it came to getting coverage for their loss or disability, they were denied. Religious affiliation was, and I believe still is, one of the most critical questions posed in applications for any type of work or amenity. Baha'is were never recognized as defenders of their country, although they did their best to save and support their motherland. Iran is the birthplace of our faith; it is a sacred place for us, and we love our country and our people, no matter how we are treated. I was almost seventeen years old when the eight-year war ended.

31

RAHMAT'S STORY

The war had been over for a few years, and most states and cities were still dealing with the effects and damages caused by it. It always takes more time to heal; constructive results always require more time and effort than destructive ones. An accident or illness can occur in one brief incident, but it may take months, years, or even forever to heal. At the end of the war years, homes had been lost, cities destroyed, loved ones killed or gone missing. The western and southern provinces faced a lot of damage, and crowds of residents of those provinces had sought refuge in Iran's central cities. The people from those provinces affected by war had nothing to go back to. War is the cruelest and most imprudent way of solving conflicts.

The pressure on the Baha'i community didn't change by the end of the war, and even during the war, there was always the risk and threat of conflict and difficulty. The Islamic clergy were still attempting to blame the shortcomings and problems resulting from the war on foreign countries, and Baha'is were always the easiest to label as spies and rebels. The law prohibits Baha'is from talking about the teachings of their faith or explaining the principles and beliefs they practice. Persecution and imprisonment, job termination, property seizure, expulsion from school, and all types of government-sanctioned denigration had become a part of our lives for many years.

Baha'is were and still are banned from government employment and higher education.

During the period when the majority of the population was struggling to meet their daily needs, Baha'is were in a worse condition. In addition to all those challenges, they had to live quietly and cautiously. There was not a single legal source to get help from. All internal media were against Baha'is, and the rulers made sure no one could hear us from beyond the borders. That much pressure, in addition to the effects of the war, was almost unbearable. In spite all the effort the rulers made to oppress us and cover our cry for help, voices started to be raised around the world in defense of the Baha'is in Iran.

Rahmat was in his twenties now. Ten years earlier, when he was only fifteen years old, he had been expelled from his school and started working like the rest of the men of the family. Even Karim dropped out of school at the age of fifteen and started to work. Rahmat was a young, intelligent, and energetic man; his blindness never seemed to be a significant disability to him. In addition to working and contributing to the family, he kept practicing his music and singing for hours each day. He also started to participate in study groups with his friends. Sometimes they could find him books written in braille.

With his angelic voice and skillful musical performance, he changed the atmosphere of every gathering he attended. His vibrant energy and his spirit of joy and confidence delighted any room he entered. He made many good friends while attending youth gatherings, and a few of them became his close friends. Almost everyone in the town knew him, as he had become one of the people ready to help with any youth event.

A few years back, when the revolution had just taken place, a few of Rahmat's close friends were arrested and imprisoned for practicing the Baha'i faith. After a few months of captivity, they were executed in a Shiraz prison. Rahmat went through a period of depression and sorrow over the loss of his best companions. I witnessed numerous times when he was praying and crying silently, even whispering, "Why didn't they choose me? Why do I get to stay and suffer after you guys?" It was so hard to watch him mourning so deeply, especially because, being blind, crying was not a comfortable action for him. I just cried with him quietly, hoping he didn't notice my presence. He was my older brother, and I looked up to him.

It took Rahmat a few months to get out of that grieving state of mind. I don't know how, but suddenly a current of energy and urgency, or perhaps a sense of obligation and mission to his faith and people, made him rise again. A spirit of sacrifice made him even more determined than before. He started going out to do home visits every day. He went to the homes of people who were affected by all types of difficulties. He prayed with them, listened to them, cried with them, talked to them, sang songs to them, and played music for them; he comforted them by assuring them that these days would pass and their pain and suffering would end. He told them their patience and strength would make a big difference in history and in the process of obtaining peace for our people; their strength and endurance would raise understanding for the need to eliminate the violence and racism.

He didn't care how far away those people lived or how hard they were to reach. He would set out alone to visit them and find their address in any part of the city. Whether it was an elderly couple who had no one left, a young couple who had difficulty coping with their life, or youth who were lost during all the changes and alterations, he was there. He spent the majority of his time visiting people who were dealing with poverty, loss, injustice, and sorrow. He just knocked at their door and spent time with them. He had an excellent connection with youth, and he was always ready to participate in their gatherings, perform music for them, or just connect.

Very soon he became a skillful motivational speaker. He was invited to towns and cities all around the country. It didn't surprise us anymore to hear he was in northern Iran or southern Iran. Our family barely saw him. He came home just occasionally for short visits. Even during those short visits, he would still have many visitors. They mostly came to invite him or take him to various activities in several towns. I remember one day, almost thirty minutes after his arrival at home, one of his friends came to take him to Isfahan. Baba got so upset, and he said to Rahmat's friend, "Hey, we are his family, and we need to spend time with him too."

It was so awkward to see Baba talk to a guest in our home in that manner. Baba loved all of us dearly, but he had a special affection and respect for Rahmat; we all knew that. He then told the friend in a softer voice, "I am his father, and I miss him too." Rahmat didn't leave for Isfahan until the next day.

There are always people who judge your actions, no matter what your intention is. People see things from different angles, and that's OK. Rahmat's work and sacrifices didn't make sense to some people, even some of our extended family members. Of course, they didn't walk in his shoes and couldn't comprehend the world from the perspective of a young blind man, a man who observed and understood everything with spiritual sight rather than the sight of his nonfunctioning physical eyes. Some people who didn't know Rahmat's journey couldn't comprehend the reason behind his selflessness and joyful spirit. They would often make discouraging statements to him. They told him many times, "You spend so much time traveling and visiting others so you don't have to deal with your own problems and obligations." Statements like that bothered him. He would come home and spend days in silence and meditation and playing music. He would feel better afterward and soon would be out visiting again. Nothing could stop him.

After finishing high school, I started working at the front desk of medical lab. Working there was safe so long as my employer didn't know I was Baha'i, and I was not planning to say anything unless they asked. We could find jobs at private practices, but if for any reason they wanted to know about our personal life or religious belief, we felt obligated to tell the truth. There was always a chance of losing your job, but on the other hand, it was a chance to tell them about the Baha'i faith and break the taboo of talking about it. When they got to know you and felt safe around you, it was less risky to talk about the faith, although they often were afraid of getting in trouble with the government for hiring a Baha'i.

Golara had married and moved to Tehran a few months before, and I had been working at the lab for a few months when one morning as I was getting ready for work, I saw Rahmat getting his suitcase ready. He said he was going to Zahedan the next day. Zahedan is the capital city of Sistan and Baluchistan Province in southeastern Iran. A friend of Rahmat's was coming to pick him up in a few hours. I wished him good luck and a safe return.

He called to me and asked me to stop getting ready for a few minutes and walked with me to the front door. He held my face softly with both hands and whispered, "Can I ask you something?"

"Yes, of course," I said.

"I want you to pray for me."

"I always do." I had watched the conflicts and struggles he dealt with for many years. I knew he was tired; he had been facing so many challenges for so long, and I was always concerned something would happen to him. The burden he was carrying on his shoulders would have been severe even for a person with no vision disability.

I experienced a weird feeling, and I told him, "This is just another trip, Rahmat *jon*" ("Rahmat, dear"). "Take it easy, and try to relax. I'm sure you will be back home safe, and we can read books together again." We had both signed up for the same study circle. Rahmat didn't have access to many books written in braille, so I read books for him, and he helped me to comprehend tough concepts. We became reading buddies.

"You know," he said, "this trip is different, and I just want to make sure I talk to you before leaving!"

I kissed him, hugged him, and promised him that I would keep him in my prayers. Then I left for work.

That conversation was really unusual, and at the same time, it felt so foreboding. But I finished getting ready for work and left for the lab. Rahmat left a few hours later.

Our parents had always had concerns about Rahmat traveling. They had talked to him numerous times and asked him to limit his travels, but he was a grown man, and he had made up his mind to do it. Even if he decided to stay in town for a short period, he would get calls and requests to visit from various cities and towns.

A few weeks had passed when I came home from the morning shift one day and saw Karim waiting with his motorcycle at the corner of our street. It was a short walk from there to our home. I was late, and I could see Mama waiting at the door. I thought Karim was there to give me a quick ride home. Karim seemed to be nervous. He said to me anxiously, "I need to tell you something, but don't show any reaction, because Mama is watching us at the end of the street. I think something has happened to Rahmat."

"How do you know?" I asked.

"Reza just said that he got a call from Uncle Rahim. Rahmat is in the hospital. Reza has gone to get Uncle Habib to come to our house to get our parents ready for the news."

That last conversation I had with Rahmat before he left crossed my mind, and I became nervous that his condition was serious, but it was too soon to form any conclusions. I got on Karim's motorcycle, and he dropped me at home.

"Why did you two stop in the middle of the road, talking?" Mama asked. "Is everything OK?"

"Yes," Karim said. "We were early. I just waited for us to come home together." He then went out for another short ride. I could see Mama had uneasy feelings. She went out to see where Karim was going, and I followed her.

Karim met Reza almost at the same spot where he'd picked me up. Uncle Habib, Aunt Mehri's husband, was on the back of Reza's motorcycle. We saw all three of them get off the bike and spend a few minutes talking. Mama said, "I don't know what Habib is doing here at this time of the day. What are they talking about? I hope everything is OK." She then asked me, "Did Karim say anything to you?"

I had nothing to say. We then saw both my brothers leaning on each other's shoulders and Uncle Habib holding them, trying to comfort them. I knew for sure then Rahmat was not in the hospital.

Baba was almost seventy-five years old, still mentally sound and physically strong, but he was tired, too tired! Yet he shoved his sleeves up and started to secure the stones and rocks for Rahmat's grave without saying a word or shedding even tear. Drops of sweat were falling down his forehead and neck. It was strange to see him working like he was working on a construction project. His emotions seemed to be entirely blocked at that point. Baba loved all of us dearly, and Rahmat was especially precious to him. He couldn't tolerate a simple scratch on us, but now he was burying Rahmat with his own hands, showing almost no feeling. Mama seemed to know what her man was doing. She was watching him and crying silently. She didn't say anything to Baba; it was a very blurred and confusing moment.

We were in the middle of Kavir-e-Lut, or Lut Desert, a vast salt desert between the provinces of Kerman and Sistan Baluchistan. It's the world's twenty-seventh-largest desert, with an area of forty thousand kilometers. I don't think there is any need to describe the condition of the climate and the soil of that desert, especially in late July.

The accident had happened in the early morning five days before. The bus had left Zahedan for Shiraz and crashed into a commercial truck coming from the opposite direction. This deadly collision happened at the border of Sirjan, a city in Kerman Province. We went to Sirjan the morning after we heard the news. The reports said the truck driver had fallen asleep, and the tragedy cost both drivers their lives, plus the lives of seven other people in both vehicles, including Rahmat's.

The imam Jema'ah, the leading clergy of Friday congregational prayer in Sirjan, would not approve and allow the burial a Baha'i person there. In their view, Baha'is are considered *najes*, unclean, and can contaminate the whole cemetery, dead or alive. That's why it took us two more days to get the approval for Rahmat's burial. Imam

Jema'ah said the only place he could let us place Rahmat to rest was an isolated spot in the middle of the sandy Lut Desert.

He sent a few of his men with a truck carrying the casket, and we walked behind that truck. Walking on those hot, salty sands was one of the longest journeys of my life. At some point I took my shoes off and decided to walk barefoot. The sand was too hot, but I tried to feel and connect with it. I was hoping I could make a bond, a trust with that abandoned part of the earth. I was about to entrust my beloved brother to that desert.

The burial was simple and quiet. Some of our Muslim relatives arrived from Neyriz. They were in awe to see, after all the years of hardship and difficulties, that Baba was still standing determined for his faith. You could see Baba was making a deep personal commitment with his young son—a man-to-man covenant, a father-and-son promise. Baba was so proud of Rahmat, and he was honored to do this last service for him. I could even imagine Baba's very personal conversation with Rahmat as he worked silently around his grave. He was telling him how grateful he was to be his father and how proud he was of his sacrifices, his service, and his loving, caring spirit toward everyone he knew. I could also imagine that Baba asked him for forgiveness for his disability, for the trials and troubles he had to face as a Baha'i child, for losing the chance to continue his education, for working like a man since he was fifteen years old, and for all the struggles he had to face alongside the family. Baba was not talking to an average man or just his son. He was talking to someone extraordinary, someone who took his God-given mission so seriously at that young age and who was transitioning to eternity now.

Rahmat was not an ordinary individual. Ordinary people don't live and die like that. Seeing a seventy-five-year-old man bury his young blind son in the middle of that hot, violent desert, securing rocks around his grave while knowing he would never be able to visit that tomb again, was something beyond vision. I think it's called faith.

The next day we walked back to that spot to say farewell to Rahmat for the last time, but we couldn't find his grave. It was not an easy search; there was nothing but sand. We didn't even know which direction to go in the middle of that nowhere. A sense of loss and being lost consumed us; it was such a heavy emotion. We were looking for Rahmat's grave behind streams of tears. At one point Mama started to call him loudly like she was waiting for his reply, and we all followed her, calling Rahmat loudly in the middle of nowhere. That was the moment we all broke down. Only God could see and hear us. I hope no one ever goes through that experience, ever. I don't remember how long we walked and cried around that hot, sunny desert. We couldn't find any sign of him. They say the desert can mess up your mind, and I got to experience that and know it is true. A strong wind had blown the night before and changed the surface of that Sahara, leaving no sign of Rahmat's resting place.

Khosrow, a firefighter who was helping us through the burial process, had witnessed our situation. He kindly offered his house to us for that night, and we accepted his offer. He had an amazing wife and four beautiful children. They did their best to make us feel comfortable at their home. Reza and Khosrow became good friends in later years.

The next day we were waiting for our bus to pick us up and take us back to Shiraz. We were so tired. The past couple of days felt like a strange dream; we were still in a state of shock. Everything had happened so quickly. It was so confusing; Rahmat was gone and had left no sign of himself in this dusty world, as if he had never even lived on this planet. We were in a strange region looking for our brother amid a remote desert. I wished many times it was a dream and we could wake up from it.

We got Rahmat's belongings. In his suitcase there was a recorded tape of his last music performance, and a picture of Abdu'l-Baha. Rahmat had been scheduled to see Dr. Khoda-Doost, a famous optical surgeon back in Shiraz. That doctor had given him slight hope that he might be able to gain sight in one of his eyes through a corneal transplant. Rahmat was not so excited about it. Perhaps he had seen enough of this world, even without the power of physical vision.

A good friend of his who was one of his hosts in Zahedan had given him the picture of Abdu'l-Baha as a gift and suggested he take it with him so it would be the very first picture he ever saw.

The recorded tape contained a few songs; they were so profound, so meaningful. It seemed Rahmat had left us a message about the purpose of his life and the meaning of his death. Rahmat had completed his mission on this earth, and he was ready to go home.

Uncle Rahim and a few of our relatives came from Neyriz. Our uncle revealed another part of Rahmat's strange journey that sent chills through our spines. Among his personal belongings we found his traveling ticket. His seat number was seventeen, which was in the fifth row of the bus, where the other passengers had had minor to medium injuries, but Rahmat was found in the front part of the bus. We asked why Rahmat had been sitting in the first row. Had the impact been that severe? Uncle Rahim said a young woman had told the investigator that a few hours before the accident, Rahmat had switched his seat with her and her little baby. She had been sitting in the first row behind the driver, but it seems the baby had been crying and making it uncomfortable for his mama and the driver. The young mother asked if anyone was willing to switch seats with her, and Rahmat offered his place to them. A few hours later, the bus encountered that trailer truck. The young mother and her baby survived, but Rahmat was gone.

Rahmat was a legendary man. He lived, served, and died like a legend. His love for Baha'u'llah, the founder of the Baha'i faith, and the desire to practice his teachings made Rahmat leave no signs or traces of himself behind, only an honorable name and good memories. That's the true meaning of life. "The heart revived by the spirit of love will never die."

This is a translation of the last poem he left for us.

> *Del bordi az man be yaghma…*
> *You plundered the land of my heart,*
> *Oh my beloved!*

Have you realized?
Oh my admired one,
What your love has done to me?
Your love nested in my heart
Refreshed and enlightened my spirit.
Polished and shined
The mirror of my soul.
So vibrant, so bright!
In your presence
My soul became delicate
And my heart, fragile.
In your absence
My soul was desperate
Just like an arrow
Ready to depart
From a bow.
The universe cannot endure
The gravity of your love
How do you expect
My weak body to stand it?
Your love flew me away,
On the winds of eternity.
Your love!
My ashes…
Your love!
My ashes…

32

MARRIAGE AND FAMILY

Rahmat's death has had a significant influence on my life, even until today. I can positively say it changed my life's direction. I am not sure which course my life would have taken if Rahmat had lived, but he passed away at the most crucial stage of my lifetime, when I was about to make important decisions. I am grateful for all the tests and trials that God placed on my path in the years following Rahmat's death, for those tests made me a stronger person, and I am thankful for my two beautiful children and honest, hardworking husband.

Like most people, we have had some bumps on our road. I couldn't comprehend some of them until many years later. My husband had to go through a similar journey living at the same time and through the same trials during the Islamic Revolution and Iran–Iraq War. He became the head of his household at the age of sixteen when his father lost his life falling off a roof on a cold December night in Shiraz. His father had worked as a security guard for a construction company. One morning they found his lifeless body face down on the ground where he had fallen, having suffered a blunt injury on the back of his head. We are still not sure if it was an accident or an act of hate. There is still no legal source from which we can get the answer and closure even today. The family had a hard time burying him.

In the eyes of the Iranian Islamic rulers, Baha'is are considered infidels, and the taking of infidels' blood is permissible. My husband's father left behind his five-months-pregnant wife and three children. Even talking about his death was hard for my husband. After twenty-five years of marriage, my husband told me the story about how he had to deal with his father's death. This is how he describes it:

"One early morning a construction worker found my father's body lying face down on the ground. He reported the incident to the authorities, but they didn't conduct an investigation, although there was a significant injury at the back of his head. They said he had probably gone on the roof to check for rain leakage, his foot slipped, and he fell. They suggested to us that we not to push the case or make any inquiries. A couple of days later, we got a call to pick up his death certificate and his identity booklet, which had been handed to the authorities.

"My mother was the only adult in the household. She was pregnant, and she was not comfortable going there, since she had two other young children at home. I said I could go. Although she was not comfortable sending me, she eventually agreed. We had lost our father already, and as the eldest child of the household, I couldn't imagine losing my mother too. I was a sixteen-year-old boy anyway, and I didn't think the authorities would have much to say to me.

"When I arrived at the address, I was surprised to see it was the location of the Baha'i center of Shiraz. I knocked at the gate, and a soldier opened the little window they'd made in the door. He asked a few questions and then let me in. He directed me to go to the last room alongside the gardens. Walking through that long yard, I felt so fearful for my life. The energy, the vibe, created an uncomfortable atmosphere. The place felt so strange now.

"When I got to the last room, I saw one of the Revolutionary Guard officers sitting behind his desk. He asked me the reason I was there, and I said I had come to get my father's death certificate. He asked, 'Doesn't anyone older than you live at your home who could come here?'

"I replied, 'My mother is not feeling well, and I have little siblings. She couldn't leave them.' He then asked for my father's name, and I gave it. That officer looked at me furiously, as if he knew something about my baba. He opened his drawer, and among many papers, he found my father's death certificate and his identification booklet. He then grabbed a red pen. I thought he probably wanted to void the ID booklet, but he didn't just do that. He started to draw a line on my father's picture with that red pen with such force that it created a big scratch across my father's face. He kept looking directly into my eyes without even blinking. It seemed he enjoyed it, and he was trying to irritate me. I could tell he was waiting for my reaction. I just watched him quietly. He drew another line scratching that photo calmly and slowly and kept staring directly into my eyes. I just waited there until he made many scratches on my father's picture and then threw the booklet in front of me on the desk.

"I just thanked him, picked up the ID booklet and the death certificate, and left. I knew if I showed any reaction or emotion, they would cause me trouble. I didn't want to create any more problems for my mother.

"On the bus back home, I took another look at my father's picture. Looking at those scratch lines, especially seeing his innocent eyes behind those cruel scratches, made me feel so violated. I was so mad, but I had to be patient. I just cried silently, and I knew it was the last time I would cry like a child. There was no place left for my childhood. I knew I had to grow up soon, and controlling my emotions seemed to be a good strategy to protect myself.

"My little sister was born four months later. She brought joy to our family, but we missed our father even more. A few weeks later, we got word from neighbors that the town's clergy had planned to demolish our home while we still lived there. We couldn't take the risk, so we left that place shortly after. It took us three years to settle down. We went from place to place, but nowhere was peaceful and safe."

Going through those years of pressure and persecution, especially watching his mother and his little sisters' struggles after losing their father and their home, being mistreated, and facing many other issues made my husband a strong and strange man, almost a coldhearted man. I will not tell you more of his personal life. I just wanted to share an example of how our tests and trials can contribute to our personalities and influence our character as humans. Those challenges can even change the definition of essential elements, even something like love.

A few years into our marriage, when we moved to the United States, I noticed my husband transform from that tough, quiet man into a loving, caring, sensitive person. He had always been an excellent provider and a loyal man wholly committed to his family, but he never let his emotions get in his way, and he was cautious not to show extra affection toward anyone.

I asked him once, "Why have you changed so much recently, and why was it so hard to show emotions and passions before?"

He replied, "Because we are safe now." I looked at him, puzzled. He said, "When I witnessed my two younger sisters suffering because of the loss of our father, especially the four-year-old, who remembered our father clearly, I decided not to let my family be so emotionally attached to me. I knew there was always a chance that I would experience the same fate as my father. I didn't want my children to suffer in case something like that happened to me."

I recalled that the only request he'd made of me at the beginning of our marriage was for me to be an independent woman and not to rely on him for anything. I had found it strange at the time, but now that we were out of that rough stage of our lives, I better understood the reason he asked that of me. I don't know if that attribute is called detachment, fear, protection, or a survival mechanism, but as strange as it was, it helped us, and I am glad that I became an independent woman.

Having told you this story, I believe today, after twenty-six years of marriage, that love is not always about displaying our emotions in public and revealing our excitement to others. In some circumstances it's safer to conceal our feelings and remain silent but still give our love a life through our actions, like my husband did throughout our marriage. I think it's complicated to hide your affections from your loved ones. At least I know I am not good at that.

Our life's direction took a complete rotation eight years into our marriage. We had two beautiful children. Our son was almost six years old, and he was getting ready to go to school soon. Our daughter was only ten months old; she was still young, but we knew the years would pass by quickly, and her education would soon be our concern. Imagining our children going through the same rough journey throughout school, work, and later in life made us fearful for their future. We were so tired, and we couldn't afford to run or fight for our lives anymore. Imagining our children going through the same trials as we had, and also dealing with other serious issues, our thinking turned in the direction of leaving our homeland, although it was not our hearts' desire. So we sold our home and all our belongings and left Iran in a matter of two weeks.

33

IMMIGRATION TO THE UNITED STATES

W e left our homeland with two young children. My husband was thirty-four years old, and I was twenty-eight. We lived in Turkey for nearly a year, waiting for the approval of our immigration to the United States. We rented a small basement in Nev-Shehir. The people of Turkey were very kind and respectful. Although we couldn't communicate at the beginning, our landlord and neighbors treated us very well and kept talking to us to the point where we learned Turkish in a matter of a few months. We were not fluent, but we could get the main idea of what they were saying.

Our landlord, Anna, her only son, Mehmet-Abi, and her daughter-in-law, Saliha, were the kindest people I had met in so long. My husband started working as a cast-iron welding technician, and I stayed home, taking care of our children. We faced no significant issues there, considering what we had gone through in our homeland. Of course, there were some financial issues and cultural barriers, but they were not big deals. After almost a year had passed, we got approved to move to the United States as refugees. Given my experience living as a citizen back home versus being called a refugee overseas, I felt safer being a refugee. This was the second time we had both lost everything, but we knew we could get through it easily this time.

Our airplane landed at a New York City airport on the morning of February 21, 2001. We collected our luggage and waited for the immigration agent to meet us. It was past 1:00 a.m., and we were exhausted. We put our bags down against a wall and sat on the floor. I had our baby girl on my lap, and our son was sitting between my husband and me. We had no idea what our next day would look like. Our son sensed our doubt and uncertainty, and he said, "Mama, can I ask you a question?"

I said, "Yes, of course my dear."

He asked with concern on his little face, "Have we become homeless now?"

My husband and I looked at each other and didn't know how to respond to his question. It was heartbreaking to see our son expressing the same fear again. Trying to hide my tears, I smiled at him, tapped his little shoulder, and told him, "Of course not. We will work and build a beautiful life together. You and your sister will go to school and will have a bright future here." I had the distinct feeling that I was telling him the truth.

The immigration agent arrived and transferred us to a smaller plane to Virginia. We saw my sister Parvin and her family waiting for us when we arrived at Dulles Airport. They had prepared two big baskets of toys and kids' treats, and my children loved them. They felt so pleased and welcomed.

Parvin and her family had moved to the United States a couple of years before us. We spent the first few weeks at their home. My husband was able to find a job as a mechanical technician in a matter of a couple weeks, and we got an apartment close to his job. Little by little we were able to collect household items. But I wasn't very comfortable communicating with people yet. I thought, if my own people back home, who shared the same language and culture with me, could treat me so wrongfully, for what reason and under what guarantee would people here in the United States accept me? They had a totally different language and culture, and they had the right to be protective of them. I believed there would be more challenges, and it was my job to get my children and myself ready for possible conflicts we might face in this new place. For a few weeks, I didn't feel comfortable enough to leave the house.

One month after our arrival, I decided to register my son for school. I knew only a few words in English, and I had not had any conversation with an English speaker yet. I grabbed my dictionary and wrote a couple of simple sentences to repeat when I got to the school. I was so afraid of making mistakes, and I was hoping they wouldn't ask any questions that I didn't understand. I just had these two sentences ready: "Good morning, I am new here. I need to sign up my son for school."

I practiced the two sentences a few times out loud. Then I got my children ready and headed out to school. When we got there, I waited for a few minutes, observing other parents' interactions and conversation with the office staff. Boy, they spoke so fast! I thought I could never talk like them in a million years—and of course, I still don't.

I waited for those parents to leave, and then I walked cautiously to the front desk. A middle-aged lady was behind it. She had short gray hair, and she smiled at me. I said good morning, and then spoke the two sentences that I had prepared. She started to talk to me, and I replied with embarrassment, "Sorry, I don't speak English."

With a reassuring smile, she asked, "What language do you speak?"

This sentence was easy to understand. I said, "Farsi!"

"Your English is much better than my Farsi," she said.

You may have heard this statement numerous times. It may sound like a typical or even trite statement, but for someone who needs to hear it at the right moment, it is salvation. At that moment I knew I had finally found a place I could call home. She accepted me! Can you believe it? She didn't even care who I was and what I believed in. It was that simple! I thought, "I have come to a place where I don't have to hide my identity or run away anymore." The best part was that my children wouldn't have to go through the trial of bigotry and persecution that my husband and I had.

The woman introduced herself as Ms. Martha. I will treasure the memory of that dialogue as my very first conversation in English, and

I will remember that wonderful woman for the rest of my life. She took time to explain the process of registration, and I found that communicating with people is not that difficult when you connect with them.

By her simple statement, by taking time to talk to me, and by her unique character, I can clearly say she broke the chain of fear and uncertainty inside me. I was a more confident woman after that brief conversation, and for that I thank her and the many other people I encountered in the following years of my life here.

I saw Ms. Martha in a gathering last year when we threw a surprise retirement party for a coworker. Ms. Martha happened to be my coworker's close friend. At that meeting, they asked me to say a few words. I mentioned my first encounter with Ms. Martha, and I said that I wasn't surprised to see they were good friends, as they both shared the same personable character. I concluded my speech with this phrase: "What you do matters!" I even have a bumper sticker on my car promoting that phrase. I got it from Holocaust Museum last year.

34

THE REASON I WROTE THIS BOOK

In addition to the personal commitment and obligations I felt to write this book, and also the encounters I had with people who encouraged me to share my story on different occasions, this is a good chance for me to share my gratitude and appreciation to many people for many reasons. If you were a part of this story or are just reading it, if you paid attention to it or disregarded it, supported me or disagreed, I thank you. If you liked this story or hated it, if you for any reason contributed a part of your life to mine through this book, positively or negatively, I thank you, because hardship and hate made me a stronger person, and love nourished my soul. We all need both of those forces in life to keep us moving.

I thank all and everyone who gave us a helping hand throughout our journey when we needed help. I thank those who could have judged us and mistreated us but chose to act according to human decency and their kind hearts. I thank the Americans for opening your homes and hearts to us, for your patience, for your generosity, and your kindness. Thank you!

To those who couldn't agree with us and acted based on the wrong information they had, what happened in the past belongs to the past, and we hold nothing against anyone. We don't need to drag our past into our future. Love and forgiveness are the primary elements of the Baha'i faith, and without these two qualities, we can never build a peaceful future for our children. Who knows? When the right time comes, all the people who had to leave Iran for various reasons may go back and rebuild our county hand in hand, without looking to our differences. We share the same love, respect, and honor for our motherland, no matter what we believe or what we have been through. We will work together to start a better future for our home. As a matter of fact, we are the children of one father if we genuinely believe in him!

Someone asked me once, "How do you feel about those who put you and your family through so much hardship and suffering for years?" I responded immediately, without a pause or a second thought, "They are innocent! They acted based on the information they had; they were just misled into the wrong direction! We have nothing against them, and they are forgiven already." Even I was surprised by my answer. I had never thought about that question before. After I gave it a second thought, I still felt that I gave the right answer.

I am so grateful and happy that talking about the Baha'i faith is not a taboo in the media anymore, and more and more human rights activists, journalists, moviemakers, civil rights activists, and even lawyers are open to breaking the silence about the years of injustice and discrimination. Thank you for defending your innocent brother and sisters.

To children and young immigrants, your parents might have never told you their stories. Perhaps they didn't want to upset you or disturb your peace and add to your challenges while you were growing up in your host country. Think about the reason you are here. Why did your parents leave their homeland and their loved ones and end up in a foreign land? You are probably here for a significant reason, and you owe it to them, and to yourself to investigate the truth about yourself and study your roots. If your parents' goal for their children was higher education, you need to start working on that. If it was for your safety and security, you need to choose a safe lifestyle and plan your future based on sound and decent decisions. If they are here for freedom and democracy, you need to stay away from taking political sides. And be open to hearing all different ideas and viewpoints, no matter where they come from. If they saved you from discrimination and violence, it's your duty to stand against racism, and spread love, respect, and tolerance. Do not let the actions of others mislead or discourage you from the right direction.

You are not here solely for pleasure; you are here for a purpose. Search for it and act upon it. Living according to your purpose will ultimately give you the real pleasure that lasts forever. And always keep in mind, no one is responsible for your success or failure but yourself! It's unlikely that you are here for the wrong motivation, but God forbid, if that's the case, you need to reevaluate your drive and reconsider your actions in the right direction. That will give you and others peace of mind and a chance to build a better world and future.

Try to search for happiness rather than fun. Pay attention to the definition of these two words. Happiness is a more profound, pure joy within your heart. Fun is usually produced by some event or activity outside of your mind and body, and in some cases, it can be false or even harmful. Happiness is an inner feeling of gratification caused by our own achievements, while fun is a temporary sense of satisfaction with little or no root in your heart. Fun can be a false pride in what we have, while happiness is a permanent feeling that makes us proud of who we truly are.

There is no pride in living in a bubble and staying safeguarded. Be proud of stepping out of your comfort zone and of the lessons you learned, even from the mistakes you made. But keep in mind this famous quote: "A mistake repeated more than once is a decision." Be mindful of choosing friends you associate. Real friends lift you and cheer you to learn more and grow to become a better person. Doubt those who hold you back or drag you down. Lastly let me tell you a secret, a code to unlock and win the real game! Never lose the attitude of learning. Life gets boring and feels empty when you stop learning. Being passionate about discovering new things opens doors of opportunity and wisdom to you. Try to learn something new every day, and you will see the mystery behind life's original game.

I am sure if your parents had decided to write their life stories, there would be thousands of books out there with similar stories.

This was just a glimpse of what my generation had to go through and why they saved you from all those troubles. Now you owe it to your future to start searching for your own truth and study your own roots. After all, what parents can't teach with love and compassion, life will teach with hardship and conflicts. It's your call!

Don't be afraid of difficulties. I read this statement today, and I don't know who the author is, but I think it is true: "When you are in a dark place, you think you are buried, but you are actually planted."

One of my high school friends sent me a video this morning. Thanks to social media, we were able to find each other after twenty-eight years. I am going to quote and share the story of that video. You decide if you agree or disagree.

"In the middle of a beautiful city, there was a museum. The floor of the museum was laid with marble tiles, and at the center of the foyer, there was a beautiful marble statue. Many people from all around the world visited the museum, and they admired that beautiful statue. One night, one of the marble floor tiles started talking to the marble statue. 'Hey, statue, we are originally from the same town. We are dug from the same mine and were transported to the same sculptor. Why then do people come here to step on me, while they praise and admire you so much? This is so unfair.'

"The statue replied, 'My dear friend and poor tile, do you remember when both of us sat there side by side in the sculptor's workshop in our original marble blocks? Do you remember how the sculptor chose to work on you first? He started using his tools on you to turn you into a masterpiece, but you resisted and started falling apart.'

"The tile replied, 'Of course I remember. I hated that man and his tools. How could he use those sharp tools on me so severely?'

"The statue said, 'That's right! When you couldn't take the pain of his tools, he gave up on you. He decided to work on me. I knew at once that if I was to become something different, I had to bear the pain. Thinking thus instead of resisting, I tolerated the pain of his sharp tools.

"'There is a price to everything in life. If you give up halfway, you cannot blame anybody for stepping on you later. Life, like a sculptor, wants to make a masterpiece of you. The question is whether you are ready to handle every test, every hardship, every trouble, every failure, and all the pain coming from its sculpting tools. Will you become a masterpiece, or will you grumble and crumble down to simply become a tile? This is what decides whether people step on you or admire you as you become a role model for others to follow.'"

35

HOW ABOUT ANOTHER RING FOR JOHN?

It was a few weeks after that summer camp in Shenandoah, and I had tried so hard to put my conversation with John out of my mind. I didn't think about him after that camp; I had too many tasks on my plate, and writing a story was not one of them. One day I encountered Kate and Bernard, a lovely couple I had known for years. They asked about my experience with the summer camp, so I gave them a brief description and shared my opinion of the camp activities.

Bernard asked me with excitement, "Did you get to meet John?"

I felt for some reason that this was a crucial question. John had already occupied my mind for a while, and I had a clear memory of my conversation with him, but I'd filed that conversation somewhere in the back of my mind and thought I wouldn't need it anytime soon. So why was this man bringing John up? Perhaps it was something like a reminder, a message, or a hint. I told Bernard, "Yes, I met John, a very extraordinary man. What is it about him? Why does he dress like that?"

Bernard laughed and said, "Ever since he became Baha'i, he has dedicated his life to homeless people. He dresses like them and helps them, especially homeless women."

"How about those many rings on his fingers?" I asked. "They look expensive!"

"For every homeless person he rescues, he buys himself a ring as a reward."

What a mind-blowing story! I was shocked.

People like John are awe inspiring. They have an open mind, an open heart, and are not afraid of asking questions or searching for certainty. I think they've found the purpose of life, just like Rahmat did.

One of my coworkers asked me once about what I believed. She asked, "What is the name of your God?" That question by itself gave me awareness about the level of our willingness or resistance to search for the truth. We prefer to set a boundary around our beliefs and not let anything add to it, generation after generation.

I asked her, "Your name is Jasmine, correct?" She nodded. "And this is a unique name your parents chose for you as part of your identification, right?" She again nodded. I continued, "Now think about the people who are related to you for many different reasons. They may call you mom, wife, sister, aunt, daughter, mentor, friend, co-worker, neighbor, and grandma. To different people you have different titles and names, but you are still the very same unique Jasmine. People refer to you by a name or a title based on their position and their perspectives. It would be unwise and wrong if they argued over your different names and titles.

"The same principle applies to God! The higher being may have different names and titles to different people and faiths, but he is still the very same unique truth that we all know and worship as humans, whether we call him God, Allah, Abba, Yahweh, Father, Yazdan, Khoda, Krishna, et cetera."

I always enjoy talking to Jasmine. We have meaningful conversations sometimes, and we both appreciate it.

We all know that humankind is at its mature stage that makes it capable of understanding this fundamental truth. The mission of all manifestations of God is not and has never been to compare or conflict with each other. Why do we even try to fight to conquer or suppress other believers of God? We are children of the same father if we genuinely believe in him.

Getting back to John's story, I am so glad I got a chance to meet him, and I am delighted that I saw Kate and Bernard after so long. They unknowingly gave me a push. I don't know if John remembers me now after almost three years. Although I was not one of the people he rescued, I think he deserves another ring. He rescued me from my fear, doubt, and uncertainty. I definitely will send him a copy of this book and a ring!

Walking on some rough trails of life, I learned not to look at the tests and difficulties as obstacles and barriers. Just like love and hate, they are powerful forces that push us to move forward, and we should acknowledge and embrace them as gates to the next chapter. Think about a time you had to deal with the gravity of a big challenge. It seemed very difficult, but eventually it opened the gate to another stage of your life. I thought I had too much on my plate already and didn't have time to do anything else, but I still managed to write my story before it was too late. I think what is important is the story we have to offer at the end. Who knew that Rahmat, a young blind man who had been laid to rest somewhere in a far desert all by himself, would influence and make changes in other parts of the world many years later? I am grateful that I was able to share his life story and accomplish one of my life missions.

36

TESTAMENT AND FINAL THOUGHT

I don't know if this story raised any questions or made you wonder why thousands of people like my family were and still are willing to go through so much hardship and face so much trouble when they could choose a less complicated faith or one that's more acceptable to practice. If you do have that question, I direct your attention to the story of every religion throughout history.

Every true religion faced the same trial during its journey, especially in the first stage of its evolution. People are not comfortable accepting change, and those who rule fight change rather than study it. But history has shown numerous times that, in the end, the truth reveals itself.

In the mid-1800s, at the time when our globe was falling into a black hole of misunderstanding and bad judgment, war and violence, invasions and slavery, Baha'u'llah, a nobleman from the land of Persia, arose to declare his mission for a better world of unity and harmony. In the Middle East, the region where Jesus the Christ was born, carried out his mission, and was crucified, another era in the history of humankind was taking shape. Its dominion spread to the Holy Land in a matter of a few years, and its influence encompassed the world in fewer than a few decades.

A new evolution in humanity, a universal vision of world civilization, accord, and peace, the coming of the promised day, was happening from east to west. Global awareness of a new world order was forming in almost every corner of the globe. Simple and unknown people who had open hearts and the clear vision to accept the new divine truth once again carried out this mission. They were preparing themselves and their children for a new age in the history of humankind. The main principles they were yearning for and working toward were and still are advanced and innovative, even for today's world. Examples of Baha'i principles include:

- Oneness of God
- All the world's religions representing one eternal and unfolding faith
- The elimination of all prejudices, meaning all humanity is one race, destined to live in peace and harmony
- The equality of women and men
- Progressive revelation
- The independent investigation of truth
- Universal compulsory education
- The development and harmony of science and religion
- Economic justice, meaning the creation of a world commonwealth of nations that will keep the peace through collective security
- The adoption of a universal auxiliary language
- The establishment of universal peace
- The Universal House of Justice

Similar to Jesus the Christ, Baha'u'llah faced trails and mistreatment throughout many years of His life. After four months of being chained in the Black Pit, He was banished from His native land. He was forced to set out even before recuperating from the ill health caused by being in the dungeon and from the wounds resulting from the weighty chains around His neck.

Fearing the spread of Baha'u'llah's word, the Persian king and Ottoman sultan worked together to exile Him to Baghdad, hoping to extinguish the flames of His call. That was the beginning of forty years of exile, further imprisonment, and persecution throughout the Persian and Ottoman Empires that ended up in the Holy Land, the land of Jesus the Christ. Just think about it! The collaboration between the Persian king and Ottoman rulers to silence His call and terminate His cause shows how significant and how prominent His message was. He returned like a "thief in the night" when the world was sleeping in the darkness of its actions.

The Baha'i World News Service shares the following statistics:

"The Baha'i faith is established in virtually every country and in many independent territories. Baha'is reside in well over one hundred thousand localities worldwide. About 2,100 indigenous tribes, races, and ethnic groups are represented in the Baha'i community. There are currently 188 councils at the national level that oversee the work of Baha'i communities. Networks of over three hundred training institutes offering formal programs of Baha'i education span the globe.

"Of the several thousand Baha'i efforts in worldwide social and economic development, more than nine hundred are large-scale, sustained projects, including more than six hundred schools and over seventy development agencies.

"There are currently ten Baha'i houses of worship—in Australia, Cambodia, Chile, Colombia, Germany, India, Panama, Samoa, Uganda, and the United States. Plans are underway to build national houses of worship in the Democratic Republic of Congo (DRC) and Papua New Guinea. Local houses of worship are also being constructed in Bihar Sharif, India; Matunda Soy, Kenya; and Tanna, Vanuatu. At the local level, meetings for worship and services are held regularly in Baha'i centers and in the homes of believers all over the world."

I think what is so unique about Baha'i houses of worship is the fact that all of them have nine entrance doors, regardless of their location and cultural designs. Those doors are meant to honor different faiths, religions, and races, a clear message to welcome everyone, regardless of their beliefs and background. This is a point in history that we can set aside our differences and work toward agreement, coherence, and unity.

The article continues, "The Baha'i international community has been registered with the United Nations as a nongovernmental organization (NGO) since 1948. It currently has consultative status with the United Nations Economic and Social Council (ECOSOC) and the United Nations Children's Fund (UNICEF), as well as accreditation with the United Nations Environmental Program (UNEP) and the United Nations Department of Public Information (DPI). The Baha'i international community collaborates with the UN and its specialized agencies, as well as member states, intergovernmental and nongovernmental organizations, academia, and practitioners. It has representative offices in Addis Ababa, Brussels, Geneva, Jakarta, and New York. Baha'i writings and other literature have been translated into more than eight hundred languages.

"Each year around one million people visit the Baha'i shrine, terraces, and gardens on Mount Carmel in Haifa, Israel. In Iran, where the Baha'i faith originated, there are now about three hundred thousand Baha'is, constituting the largest religious minority in that country."

Although Iran is the birthplace of the Baha'i faith, Baha'is have been mistreated, harassed, and persecuted for more than 150 years. Yet they still believe in their mission of making a better world for all humankind.

"The Baha'i faith is the second most widespread independent world religion. It has significant communities in more countries than any other religion except Christianity, and it is among the fastest-growing religions in the world. The members of the Baha'i faith come from virtually every nationality, religious background, ethnic group, and social class."

For more information on the Baha'i faith, please visit www.bahai.org.

YOUR THIRTY SECONDS OF SILENCE

Those long thirty seconds of silence that I had to endure as a child, on the day of Ashura was the turning point of my life's direction. I had no goal or desire to write a book about it, but you know my story now: it was a call, not a decision that I made!

When I started to write my story, I just wanted to get stuff out of my mind and off my chest to be able to focus more on my daily routine at home and at work. I knew it would be another project that I was afraid to complete. I had no plan to put myself in another unfair and disappointed position, like the way my school achievements were treated, and if I did, I knew my subconscious would kindly stop me. But it didn't! Not this time.

Back to the thirty seconds of silence. As you finish reading this book, at the end of these lines, I respectfully ask you to close this book, take a deep breath, close your eyes gently, and take thirty seconds of silence to reflect on what you just read. I hope you will be able to reflect on some points in the book and find an answer to this question: What is your call?

Thank you,

CPSIA information can be obtained
at www.ICGtesting.com
Printed in the USA
LVHW051556210221
679588LV00013B/251

9 781649 903181